The Practical Criticism of Poetry
A Textbook

The Practical Criticism of Poetry
A Textbook

by

C. B. COX & A. E. DYSON

EDWARD ARNOLD

© C. B. COX AND A. E. DYSON, 1965

First published 1965
by Edward Arnold (Publishers) Ltd.
41 Bedford Square, London WC1B 3DP

Reprinted 1966
Reprinted 1969
Reprinted 1972
Reprinted 1976
Reprinted 1978

ISBN 0 7131 5050 5

Printed in Great Britain by
Unwin Brothers Limited
The Gresham Press, Old Woking, Surrey, England
A member of the Staples Printing Group

ACKNOWLEDGEMENTS

The Authors and Publisher wish to acknowledge the kind permission given by Rupert Hart-Davis Ltd. to reprint *Here* by R. S. Thomas; The Marvell Press to reprint *Lines on a Young Lady's Photograph Album* by Philip Larkin; Faber & Faber Ltd. to reprint *On the Move* (from *The Senses of Movement*) by Thom Gunn; Harper & Row Inc. and Faber and Faber Ltd. to reprint *Six Young Men* (from *The Hawk in the Rain*) by Ted Hughes; Oxford University Press to reprint *Carrion Comfort* (from *The Poems of Gerard Manley Hopkins*) by Gerard Manley Hopkins; Macmillan & Co. Ltd. of New York, London and Canada and the Trustees of the Hardy Estate to reprint *The Shadow on the Stone* (from *The Collected Poems of Thomas Hardy*) by Thomas Hardy; Messrs A. P. Watt & Son and The Macmillan Co., New York, to reprint *Longlegged Fly* by W. B. Yeats; Faber & Faber Ltd. and Harcourt Brace & World Inc. to reprint an excerpt from *Little Gidding* (from *Four Quartets*) by T. S. Eliot; Random House Inc. and Faber and Faber Ltd. to reprint *Our Bias* (from *Collected Shorter Poems*) by W. H. Auden; J. M. Dent & Sons Ltd., New Directions Inc. and the Literary Executors of the Dylan Thomas Estate to reprint *Fern Hill* (from *Collected Poems*) by Dylan Thomas; International Authors N.V. and Horno N.V. to reprint *A Love Story* (from *Collected Poems*) by Robert Graves; Mr. Ted Hughes to reprint *Sculptor* (from *The Colossus*) by Sylvia Plath.

"To criticise is to appreciate, to appropriate, to take intellectual possession, to establish in fine a relation with the criticised thing and make it one's own".

Henry James, *Preface to 'What Maisie Knew'*

PREFACE: HOW TO USE THIS BOOK

I

This book is intended as an introduction to 'practical criticism' by the direct method. The thirty exercises are each planned to form the basis for a teaching session (though some could be prescribed for written work instead). In our view, practical criticism is best taught by discussion, and the second part of the Introduction sets out some of the problems connected with this. The first part of the Introduction is an account of the aims of practical criticism, and is designed for those who are encountering the technique for the first time. We bear in mind that some students come to it in a very wary mood.

The main part of the book is given to the thirty exercises, which might be considered in two sessions a week over fifteen weeks or, if there is not time for this, in one session a week over most of a teaching year. The first seven exercises are accompanied by our own specimen analyses, or by a record of group discussions by students we have taught. When these are used, the participants should have prepared themselves by reading and thinking about both the poem and the analysis or group discussion. We suggest that the poem should be considered first, and that the analysis or group discussion should be read only after personal impressions of the poem have been formed. One of our main purposes is to counter dogma in criticism, and we hope that students will register disagreements with the critical commentary, as well as agreement when they feel they have been helped. But the essence of this method is that agreements and disagreements should be referred to the text, and closely reasoned; they should not be regarded simply as the assertion of a differing taste. Our commentaries are followed by further questions, which might lead the discussion to new ground.

The later examples are usually followed by comment and questions, and when they are, students should consider these before the teaching session begins. One or two students might be detailed to report on factual matters, or all students might be told to prepare to report in the event of their being asked. The questions can also be used as a basis for written work, some for short exercises, some for essays of a more extended kind.

Other examples are given without any questions or comments. Here, the compiling of a critical procedure for group discussion might be one of the exercises undertaken by the student.

Naturally a book of this type cannot be comprehensive, but we have tried to bear two general principles in mind:

(i) Students who work through the thirty examples will have visited some (though by no means all) of the major English poets, and most of the representative *genres*.

(ii) There may be some occasional use in studying bad poems or bad advertisements, but in our view, the surest critical taste is formed by appreciation of what is good. Our examples are taken, therefore, from poetry that we like. Naturally not all of these examples are equally good, and discrimination remains an important challenge every time. We recognise that not everyone will share our personal likings, and that some fundamental disagreements will arise.

II

The next stage. This book is an introduction to Practical Criticism, and students will wish to proceed from it to a more advanced stage. Our *Modern Poetry: Studies in Practical Criticism* includes twenty critical analyses, all of modern poems, which could be made the basis for further group discussions; and that book also includes a short history of practical criticism from

I. A. Richards to the present time. We very strongly recommend Cleanth Brooks' *The Well-Wrought Urn*. This is an excellent book, indeed perhaps the best existing collection of critical analyses. It provides an introduction to the study of longer poems than we have used here, or in our *Modern Poetry:* and it offers a useful transition from practical criticism to critical theory. Our view is that the experience of practical criticism should come before the study of critical theory, since the second is, or ought to be, dependent upon the first.

III

Glossary. We provide at the end a very short glossary of critical terms. An excellent longer glossary is M. H. Abrams' *A Glossary of Literary Terms*, published in an 8s. paperback by Holt, Rinehart and Winston (New York). We would suggest that groups or classes using this book should have at least one copy of *A Glossary of Literary Terms* available for consultation during discussion, and that group members should find time to read it through and take notes.

Bibliography. Students of practical criticism will clearly be helped by a wider knowledge of the historical and intellectual background of English literature. We provide select bibliographies for more advanced students, with asterisks against the best books from which to begin.

INTRODUCTION

1 *Practical Criticism: What is it?*

One question often asked about practical criticism is very basic: why read poems in this way at all? Is 'analysis' not hostile to the spirit of poetry? This doubt has been expressed too often to be easily shrugged aside. Wordsworth's well-known lines are sometimes quoted:

> . . . our meddling intellect
> Mis-shapes the beauteous forms of things;
> We murder to dissect . . .

and this is prophetic, it is suggested, of the risks to which modern students of literature are exposed. Is a beautiful poem to be reduced, by the probing intellect, to its bare bones? What is to become of its beauty, its charm and spontaneity, its spiritual life?

A short answer to these doubts is that, in addition to mis-conceiving the nature of practical criticism, they underestimate the poems they appear to defend. They even suggest that our pleasure in poetry is a subjective illusion, which closer acquaintance with the poem cannot sustain. But one has only to trust poems a little to find that such fears are insulting as well as wrong. A poem that is in any degree successful blossoms under our careful attention, and comes into its fullness as we proceed. A really great poem begins, indeed, to take possession of us—not immediately, and at one bound, but insidiously and with stealth, over an unpredictable period of time. An isolated phrase, or a line or a sequence of lines, will return to us, with a strange sense of fitness and familiarity. Where did we hear that, we wonder? —it could scarcely be better put. Or it may be that we forget the poem altogether after analysing it, but coming upon it again later, we are struck by its form and beauty in an altogether new way. It is not exactly that we recall our analysis step by step, but rather that the experience of the poem's totality, its uniqueness, captures us more powerfully than before. The analysis has done its work, and the poem has proved all the stronger for it. Our reading includes a new sense of the poem's structure and imagery, its tone and verbal delicacy, its precise effects.

This move towards precision is what practical criticism exists to achieve. The practical criticism of a poem is not the opposite to enjoyment, as students new to it are apt to fear. It is not the substitution of an intellectual pleasure for an aesthetic pleasure, or the diminishing of poetic understanding to a dull routine. On the contrary, it is an opening up of the poem for what it can really be for us: a unique and fascinating experience, carefully wrought by its maker, and fully available only to those with the patience, as well as the sensibility, to recreate. If the poem is a good poem, our analysis begins in pleasure, and deepens that pleasure as we proceed. It makes our pleasure more articulate, and therefore more meaningful. Emotion is enriched and extended by the exercise of thought.

To discuss the careful reading of poems in this manner is to defend it; but is it not careless reading that should more obviously be on trial? We cannot be content to like poems merely at random, and to pay them the compliment of no more than a passing glance; we cannot be content to take from a great poem only what we were expecting from it, as though it were simply a confirmation of something we already knew. The great poem has the power to enrich and extend us, to make us something more than we were before. In its essential greatness, it is unlike any other poem we have ever read; but how is this uniqueness to reach us, unless we attend precisely and in very great detail to what it is? Every word in it counts, every interplay of metre with rhythm, every modulation and nuance of tone. The poet writing the poem has certainly been conscious of many effects he precisely intended; and this precision, for us as for him, is not the opposite to poetic experience; it is the means by which the poem is achieved. The poet, like any other artist, depends upon an audience which will follow him closely. Like Henry James in the Prefaces to his novels, he will hanker after readers who are not only sensitive and intelligent, but also trained.

So the reader has to co-operate by an active reading of what is in front of him. The poem exists after a fashion on the printed page, and between its covers on the bookshelf, but its real existence is only when in a reader's mind and consciousness it comes alive. What Ruskin had to say about 'seeing' is a useful analogy:

> The greatest thing a human soul ever does in this world is to see something, and tell what it saw in a plain way. Hundreds of people can talk for one who can think, but thousands can think for one who can see.

Ruskin's meaning is that most of us look only hazily at the world about us, noticing the things we expect to see, or are familiar with; the other things, or the finer shades of the things we do see, we either ignore, or distort into the image of what we expect. The artist, says Ruskin, is the man who really 'sees'. He looks with the utmost closeness, and perceives that no two clouds, or trees, or buildings are alike.

In literary terms, the practical critic is the man who really 'sees'. He is not content to reduce the poem in front of him to a cliché or a commonplace; he examines it until its particular reality comes vividly to life. The rewards of such attention are very considerable, since in great poems the words themselves, as well as the experience they convey, are more alive, more revealing and disturbing, than they are in the contexts of every day. 'It is very warm', we say, making the word 'warm' the merest gesture; or, 'it is very simple'—referring perhaps to Wordsworth's Lucy poems, or anything else that we think we can easily understand. But consider the words 'warm' and 'simple' in Dylan Thomas' 'Fern Hill':

So it must have been after the birth of the simple light
In the first, spinning place, the spellbound horses walking warm
 Out of the whinnying green stable
  On to the fields of praise.

'Simple' regains, here, its full vitality, as a word meaning unified, uncomplicated, and therefore invincible; it is the meaning of St. Thomas Aquinas, when he wrote of the simplicity of God. And 'warm' recreates the miracle of creation itself, the flesh-and-blood gladness emerging from coldness and chaos, to know itself triumphantly in a word. One is reminded not only of vivid moments from one's own experiences, but also of other literary usages in the past. There is Shakespeare's Leontes, for instance, in *A Winter's Tale*, when after a sixteen-year vigil of grief and torment, he is shown a statue of his dead wife; not as she used to be in life, but as she would be now, if she were still alive. The sight of the statue, so tormentingly faithful to Hermione, moves him unbearably; until against all expectation, he sees a movement in what he had taken to be stone. 'O, she's warm', he cries—and the miracle of life itself, of flesh and blood replacing the unyielding coldness, is captured in a word. It is moments like these which make the language of Shakespeare and many other great poets so marvellous. Our power to respond to them is nurtured by the training which practical criticism gives.

Basic Approach to a Poem. The purpose of this book is practical, and the various technical matters a student will have to become acquainted with—rhythm and metre for instance, diction and syntax, stanza forms and *genres*—are best learned, with the aid of the glossary, as he goes along. But for the basic approach to each poem, we suggest three main questions that ought to be kept in mind:

(i) What is it *about*?
(ii) How is it *done*?
(iii) Does it succeed?

As a further guide, we might use the word 'subject' to describe what the poem is 'about', and the term 'content' to describe what it *is*. We can then consider the poet's attitude to his 'subject', and the nature of his 'content'; and this leads on to a judgment upon the poem itself.

The distinction between 'subject' and 'content' is a clear-cut one; we suggest these terms for convenience, though obviously any other clearly defined terminology will suffice. By 'subject', we signify the poem's public meaning. The poem is 'about' religion, or love, or the fall of man, or wishing to be older or younger than one is, or a cat catching goldfish, and this is its 'subject': the concrete occasion on which it turns. The 'subject' comes straight from the poet's experience of life, and links him with all other poets and readers whose experience in any way touches his own. *Paradise Lost* is a poem 'about' God and Satan, about men and angels, and the fall of men and angels, and the redemption of men. It is also a poem 'about' Christian theology, and is near to the centre of a very important and protracted religious debate.

To establish the 'subject' of a poem in this sense is clearly important, but it does not tell us anything distinguishing about the poem itself. Anyone can write a poem on such themes, with more or less orthodoxy, and the poem may be good or bad. The 'subject' is to this degree general; and though a poet may have his personal insights or emphases, these do not necessarily distinguish him from everyone else. A paraphrase of *Paradise Lost* might be very revealing about its 'subject', but would not begin to explain why we value the poem as we do.

By 'content', in contrast to 'subject', we signify the poem itself; the unique combination of words, rhythms, images, overtones and other effects, which can be recognised as belonging to one period rather than another, and, if the poem is sufficiently distinctive, to one poet rather than another. 'Content' signifies the unique co-existence of a more or less public 'subject' with a particular and concrete aesthetic form. It is the actual set of words before us, with their qualities as an artefact which come alive for us as we read; it is the tension between a more or less normal set of ideas and experiences, and a particular, once-for-all set of words.

As critics, our primary concern will be with the poem's 'content', though its subject, which is part of its content, must clearly be understood as well. Many critics make the elementary mistake of starting with certain 'subjects' which they approve of, and making these the measure of all the poems they read. If the poem 'means' something they agree with, they say it is a good poem, if it means something they disagree with, they say that it is bad. There is a temptation, even at a fairly sophisticated level of criticism, to adopt dogmatic or prophetic standards, and to make *these* the measure of a poem's worth. Thus, some critics judge whole areas of poetry as inadmissible, simply because the poet's 'subject', or the tone and mood in which he deals with his subject, is personally offensive to them. Some Marxist critics, for instance, demand a certain kind of social theory and commitment before they will give their approval to a work of art. Certain other critics will praise a poem just because of its 'subject'. Young's *Night Thoughts* had a vastly inflated reputation for over a century largely because its highly religious and moralistic 'subject' distracted attention from its 'content' in our present sense.

The reader of poetry should bear in mind equally, then, both what the poem *says* (the paraphrasable subject), and what it *is*, the artefact that could exist in no other way. The 'subject' may be tragic or depressing, but the form may exemplify beauties or felicities which are a joy and consolation for the mind. Between 'content' and 'subject' there is a gulf which no simple moralising or philosophising can bridge; for poetry is not a translation of commonplaces or platitudes into riddles, nor is criticism the translation of riddles back into commonplaces or platitudes. The very experience with which the poem deals is heightened, yet also altered, by its form. What the poem offers us is not direct experience, but experience uniquely transmuted and refined. The poem in its own existence is also an object; and an object which may itself, like a symphony or a great cathedral, be a shaping experience upon our lives.

Two Images. We would like finally to offer two images of the critic, which seem to us useful, as long as they are not carried too far. Certain more extravagant images of the critic's rôle in society seem to us positively misleading; we cannot see him as either sage or prophet, hero or priest. Nor can we see him as a Judge presiding over perpetual sessions, a stern upholder of Standards against creative offenders, who are hauled before him to be convicted of very varied and often heinous sins. The critic *does* discriminate, and he may offer wisdom; but it is a serious dislocation when these are seen as his central—sometimes even as his sole—concerns.

Our own images are of the critic as Connoisseur, and the critic as Conductor or Producer. The critic as connoisseur may seem an old-fashioned idea, but if one can divorce it from the notion of well-to-do dilettantism and return to the dictionary definition, it still has something important to say: 'One who knows a subject well; a critical judge in art, music, etc.' The very modesty of this can be sobering at a time of critical inflation; considered in itself, moreover, it can help us to get certain priorities right. The first is that though the practical critic ought to be as precise as a scientist, he is not a scientist; the scientist moves among results which can be experimentally verified, and which can be reached by any other scientist using the same techniques of experiment, no matter how dissimilar in temperament, or belief, or sensibility he may be: but the critic's findings are inextricably connected with temperament, and belief, and sensibility, so that though he can (and indeed must) demonstrate his findings concretely, yet he cannot win assent in exactly the scientific way. If one thinks of the connoisseur of wine (say), the same balance between taste and precision will be seen. The wine connoisseur must have the widest acquaintance with his chosen field; he must be familiar with many kinds of experience; he must be able to do full justice to the rare vintages without slighting or neglecting the lesser delights. He may demonstrate his skill in recognising a wine by tasting it; and this is a proof that his skill is a valid one, even though he cannot demonstrate it by any purely scientific technique. Somewhat similarly, a practical critic might demonstrate his skill by 'dating' an unseen passage out of context; and this is a proof of his methods, even though no scientific formulation of them can be found.

The 'connoisseur' is also a concept which links pleasure in art with the idea of discipline. The connoisseur certainly enjoys art, and is unlikely to become over-censorious in his dealings with it, or to use the best as an enemy of the good. But on the other hand, he has the discipline of his considerable experience and researches behind him, so that his enjoyment does not have simply the status of a whim. The man who says 'I know what I like' is of use to his fellows only if they can trust him; and the difference between the connoisseur and the philistine is precisely the discipline in the one, conjoined with intelligence and talent, which leads other men to have this trust. The connoisseur, again, is a man with a sense of the form and structure of created objects; one who recognises that beauty is as much a character of works of art or literature as 'truth'. He is unlikely to forget Dr. Johnson's maxim that poetry instructs *by pleasing*; and he will certainly not fall into one of the besetting sins of the writers of literary history, who when confronted with diversity usually want to say 'either/or' instead of 'both/and'. This sometimes takes the form of an 'either/or' inserted between pairs of writers —Sophocles or Euripides, Webster or Jonson, Milton or Donne, Pope or Keats, George Eliot or Dickens. Or it can be an 'either/

or' between literary categories—Romantic or Classical, Symbolist or Naturalist, Traditional or Modern and the like. The critic who is a connoisseur will instinctively favour 'both/and' as a formula whenever he can. If he does prefer Pope to Keats, or vice versa, it will not be on account of the labels that other critics have attached.

A final point concerns the connoisseur's own manner. If he believes that literature is, among other things, a civilised pleasure, he will cultivate an ease of manner himself. Like the philosopher, he will hope to remain intelligible to an educated reader, however difficult the things he has to say. Above all, he will be in sympathy with the creative temperament in all its unpredictable variety, remembering that the springs of creation can be in memories of childhood or first love, in chance smells or tastes, in a few chords struck on a piano, as well as in the desire to shape moral patterns, or juggle with symbols, or solve the riddle of human life.

We suggest the connoisseur, then, as one useful image; our second, which is equally controversial, is the image of the producer or conductor; the man who produces works of drama or music and, in one place, for one audience, brings them alive. Clearly this analogy is only a partial one. In reading a poem we are on our own, in a sense, with the words in front of us; we do not need intermediaries as we do between a play and ourselves in the theatre, or between a symphony and ourselves in the Concert Hall. But *Hamlet* or Beethoven's Ninth Symphony have an ideal reality for us, even when we are not at a performance. We approach them personally through the text or the score, or perhaps just in memory; and the various performances we have seen and heard will be part of our present awareness; they will add something to what we have registered and appropriated for ourselves. In a similar manner, a critic's insights might pass into our own consciousness of the work he has written about. In a sense, he has 'performed' it; he has responded to its form and structure, its individual parts, its totality, and has passed on his findings for other readers to share. A first-rate piece of criticism is very like a 'performance'; it is a bringing alive of a work, through close and faithful attention to it, at one time and in one place.

Consider, for instance, a truly great conductor like Toscanini. His performances of Beethoven's symphonies were extraordinarily dynamic, and had upon them a stamp which could not be missed. Listening now to the records of the Ninth Symphony, one says 'Toscanini's Ninth!'—by which one does not mean 'Toscanini's Ninth *rather* than Beethoven's', but 'Beethoven's Ninth brought alive splendidly and authentically, yet in a manner which is recognisably unique'. Toscanini's performance is, of course, minute and faithful; it emerges from a prolonged and painstakingly detailed study of the score. But to this study, there has been added a personal sensibility and temperament; the recreation—or 'performance'—is precise, but not *standard*; it is not precise, to return to this important distinction, in the manner of a scientific experiment.

For ourselves, Toscanini's Ninth is a wonderfully valuable addition to our understanding of Beethoven. Our own 'Ninth' will be permanently enriched by Toscanini's, even while we recognise that it is not the only 'Ninth', and that it is not definitively the 'best' Ninth; that it is not the 'last word'. There will be other great performances, both precisely faithful to the score as Toscanini's was, and yet equally distinctive themselves. Perhaps each age will recreate all great works of art with its own insights. The performer or critic is a link in this chain of continual recreation; the chain which, perhaps over centuries, the living influence of the particular work of art will become.

There are two further analogies that might be drawn from this image, both of great importance if the critic is to understand both the value and the limitations of his rôle. Firstly, the producer or conductor is not greater than the creative artist. He exists to serve the creative artist, without whom he would have no rôle to perform. Anyone who tries to exalt the critic above the creative artist is under a grave misapprehension. The critic is not a moralist or a judge in any autonomous sense; he is a moralist and a judge only inside the province of created art. Secondly, the producer and the conductor *are* judges, but judgment is only a small, and even a preliminary part, of what they do. They may decide that a certain play, or a certain symphony, is not worth performing. If they do, they can ignore it; and no one could possibly take exception to this. But when once they have decided to produce a play or to conduct a symphony, the art of judgment takes another form. The producer of *Charley's Aunt* cannot always be saying 'this play isn't as good as *Hamlet*!', the conductor of Mozart's Fortieth Symphony cannot always be lamenting, 'if only I were conducting Verdi's *Requiem* instead!' When one is committed to a work, then one does one's best for it. The main responsibility is to recreate it—faithfully and sensitively. After this, one can return again to the larger judgments: that Bizet is less good than Berlioz, and Berlioz than Brahms. But even then, one would not give up the less great simply because there is a greater. In a similar manner, the literary critic ought to do his best to recreate precisely and sympathetically the poems in front of him *before* he rushes into a final class list of Firsts, Seconds, Thirds, Fourths, and also-ran. One has hardly to add that the work of judgment comes more reliably from a critic who has trained himself to sympathetic recreation than from one who has dogmatically decided that most literature is really not worth his time.

We suggest that students should now embark on our thirty examples, consulting the glossaries and bibliographies as they go along. The second part of this Introduction is on problems which group or class discussion might involve.

2 Teaching by Discussion: Some problems for universities and schools

The seminar is a teaching method with a long history, but the word 'seminar' still sounds foreign in English ears. 'Teaching by discussion' might be a better description, since this is what it really is. The participants sit around a table and talk with their instructor, and the teaching session—one hour, an hour and a half or two hours, occasionally longer—is spent discussing a text.

English Literature. We are not sure how most of the other disciplines are adapted to this method and cannot therefore speak of it at large. There is reason to think that some would encounter more problems than others, and that each would have quite particular problems to solve. The teacher of English Literature, however, is likely to find the method very well suited to his needs. What one gets in a seminar is an exchange of insights and responses, with the text as a fixed point in the centre, and the discussion pulling and tugging against this in every way. No single contribution can be powerful enough to carry conviction unless real demonstration and persuasion are achieved. The notion of criticism as dogma is virtually discounted; but so is the opposing error, that criticism is simply what one particular reader happens to feel. Close reading and honest heartsearching are forced upon the participants in a successful seminar by the very process which brings the text alive. The historical background has to be established, along with assumptions and conventions of the author's style; but this background is only a prelude to immediate and personal relevance, to the here-and-now of Jonson's putative 'all time'.

Liturgical Reform. As with many revolutions in basic attitude, the seminar's most obvious aspect is liturgical. The pedagogue descends from his rostrum, and seats himself among those who have come to learn. The change from the older conception of don, or of schoolmaster, is dramatic. The instructed are no longer captive and purely receptive, like so many horses brought to the water; the instructor is no longer begowned and omniscient, one whom to answer back or even question may be risky, and to catch out a rare and horrific pleasure for the bold. The participants join together, rather, in a voyage of discovery; they are free to question one another and to cross-question, but not free—this freedom is sacrificed—to refuse to take part. The instructor becomes one among others, at least for the questioning. To catch him out might even be normal, since he cannot know everything: yet not *being* caught out becomes correspondingly important, and he soon learns the need for an adequate brief.

The physical arrangement differs from a classroom or lecture hall; chairs are arranged round a table, and the instructor places himself centrally, either at one end of the table, or in the middle of one of the longer sides. If this is not possible, at least the usual classroom pattern should be broken. Chairs might be arranged in a semi-circle or double semi-circle, with the instructor in the centre, but so placed that the group can do battle over his head. The ideal student number seems to be eight or nine, with fifteen as a maximum; but if this cannot be met from teaching hours (usually it cannot), twenty or more can be handled without too much loss, especially when the seminar is based upon a manageable text.

The Instructor. The teacher's problems in seminar teaching are considerable; the conduct of seminars is an art about which he continually learns. The key problem, without any doubt, is the creation of atmosphere. The seminar has to be friendly, yet not too informal. Intellectual rigour and discipline have to co-exist with humanity and mutual respect.

In this matter, as in certain others, the seminar is difficult; more difficult that the lecture supported by tutorial, which is an altogether less exacting teaching pattern to conduct. The lecturer is mainly concerned with his material, and the ordering of this he can determine in advance. He must, of course, 'sense' his audience, and must to this extent be ready to improvise if the need should arise. But as long as the audience is interested and attentive, he can proceed more or less as he planned. He does not have to bother about members of the audience individually. If he knows them personally, then perhaps he will be aware of them, but it is a general *rapport* which most determines whether he succeeds or fails. For this reason, the lecture can also be very satisfying. A tense and expectant audience is one of a teacher's most valued short-term rewards.

In seminar teaching, the organisation is very different. The ordering of material is determined largely by the other participants, who therefore matter vitally as individuals for most of the time. How is the instructor to direct the discussion to some purpose, yet not to force it?—to bring individual members in most usefully, yet to make his own contribution without forcing the pace? Nothing can be planned in detail, or even predicted. The discussion has to be taxied into position on the runway, and prepared for take-off. Everything depends upon its rising swiftly into the air without mishap; the direction has then to be determined, as plausibly as possible, during the flight. Often, of course, such an image is altogether too optimistic to describe what happens; some seminars crawl miserably along like badly wounded animals, looking for somewhere to die. At such times, the instructor's main energy may be expended on keeping his temper, while the other participants become increasingly guilty, or miserable, or bored. Just occasionally, a seminar moves with such speed and indisputable brilliance that the instructor comes away with a glowing sense of great things achieved. But more usually, whatever achievement there is goes on under the surface. There is nothing so tangible as the attentive interest of an audience at a lecture. The long-term rewards may be even greater, but they have to be appropriated at the time by an act of faith.

This is why eight or nine is the ideal student number for a seminar. When there are more than this, the instructor will usually rely too heavily on his articulate students, and allow the shy or the lazy to lose themselves in a crowd. The shy, of course, are a particular problem; they must be helped over their shyness without being embarrassed, just as the brash or opinionated must be subdued without being crushed. The bad student can greatly overestimate his importance, and ruin a seminar; but the good student—or one sort of good student—can estimate himself much lower than he is. A very good student may be especially self-critical; he may feel less talented, less adequate, less 'clever' than his fellows; he may be unwilling to contribute unless he has something of outstanding interest to say. And here, very naturally, is the heart of the problem. In written work, such self-criticism is essential, but during seminar discussion a willingness to think aloud, to fill in gaps, to experiment, is necessary to the success of the whole. The best things, indeed, often come *en passant*: or they may come belatedly, after certain false starts have been made. It is necessary sometimes for the obvious and the commonplace to enter the discussion: as a way of approaching the subject, perhaps, or of steering it back towards course. One lives in hopes of the genuinely original; and these hopes are sometimes gratified very suddenly, taking everyone most pleasantly by surprise.

The instructor's first business, then, is to establish a proper atmosphere. No one must be made to wish he hadn't spoken, or be made to feel silly; the sarcastic and the scathing are impossible (so they should be in all teaching systems), yet standards of relevance and excellence must be clearly defined. This is why mutual trust is necessary, before the work of learning can be embarked upon. The seminar's priorities are inescapably humane.

And this is the context in which the other challenges to the instructor offer themselves: to keep the discussion moving without disrupting it; to make his own contribution where it most appropriately fits. Perhaps his main problem is posed by facts and information: where do these fit in, and how far can the discussion proceed usefully until they do? In our own view, facts and information fit best into lectures; and a pattern of one lecture to every two seminar discussions, such as is being developed in the School of English Studies at the University of East Anglia, may offer the best solution. The instructor has, however, to organise his own opinions and insights. No seminar discussion of any poem or novel will ever resemble another, and opportunism, unsupported by the encouraging attentiveness of an audience, is therefore endlessly required. It is more important for a seminar to flow smoothly than for it to be inclusive; yet it is equally important for it to flow deep, without flooding its banks.

The Students. The demands upon the instructor are therefore considerable; but there are unusually heavy demands upon the students as well. There is no spoon-feeding in a seminar system, no concession to note-taking; there is nothing which can be transferred with reverence to a notebook, and transcribed more or less accurately in the exam. The student cannot see himself, even if he wishes to, as passive; certainly he cannot sit back waiting and expecting to be entertained.

To put this another way, the student has much more than the usual opportunity to sabotage education. If he wants to—or even if he does not want to, but has just been lazy—he can make the system impossible to work. The seminar method presupposes his active co-operation, his willingness to read and to think about the texts upon which each session is to be based. If he has not read 'the book', he can sit through a lecture; he can even get something of value out of the lecture, though not as much as if the reading had been done. But if he has not read the text prescribed for a seminar, there is little point in his attending. He cannot contribute to the discussion, and he cannot learn.

The basic need then is that he should have read the text; and that he should have read it recently, and closely, rather than in any more distant or haphazard way. It is not enough for him to have enjoyed an illustrated Walter de la Mare in the nursery; nor is it enough, though this may be less apparent, for him to have spent a term on Walter de la Mare a year or so before. It is not enough for him to have skimmed through 'The Eve of St. Agnes' in the last day of a holiday, nor is it enough for him to have read one or two stanzas of 'The Eve of St. Agnes' the evening before. One might argue that *any* worth-while English course presupposes recent, close reading; but there is a sense in which the seminar presupposes this more than any other teaching method, by forcing the student to confront openly and publicly the depth and complexity of his response.

There are further stresses and strains for the student, some of them arising from the competitive nature of the examination at the end. One of the more honest university students we have taught brought a very formidable one straight into the open, on the principle that it ought not to be deemed too disreputable to discuss. If one puts all one's best ideas into the public kitty, she wondered, how is one to be sure of getting credit for them at the proper time? Since examinations are what we know them to be, isn't some form of discreet secrecy, some holding of a final strength in reserve, the very essence of prudence? And in other teaching systems, such a dilemma seldom presents itself to the student. He meets his fellow students in ones or twos for discussion, at weekly tutorials; but even here, his best ideas are probably well hidden in an essay, which only the tutor will have read. He hoards his small but growing store of insights for the Final Examiner, hoping that when these privileged eyes at last behold them they will glitter just that degree more spectacularly than all the other hoarded stores. The seminar method at least shatters the (unstated?) assumptions behind *this* situation, in favour of shared insights in a voyage of mutual discovery and good will. Yet the examination cannot be wholly disregarded; and perhaps a course-credit system is helpful or desirable, if students are to feel that their own contributions are really credited to them in the end.

Personality. The seminar system brings into teaching the personality of the participants, including the instructor; and this seems to us to represent a valuable gain. Since most of us have convictions on such matters as religion and politics, one of the silliest and most self-defeating of conventions is that these should not be allowed to 'obtrude'. Of course they will obtrude, whatever one teaches; but if one teaches literature, the judgment of values, and of imaginative experience, forces them into relevance for much of the time.

It is important that the teacher should be explicit and honest about his beliefs, for at least two reasons. The first is that since they will colour his judgments anyway, it is better to have them in the open, so that students can inspect and if need be discount them, than that they should operate as an insidious assumption in his tone. It is notorious that if you refuse to state your extra-literary assumptions, you can gain a spurious universality for them behind the scenes.

The second reason is that education is a process devoted to developing individual judgment and personality; and this is not helped if every matter of genuine importance is regarded as too controversial to be discussed. We are all aware of differences of political and religious allegiance among our contemporaries. We want to guard, certainly, against any teacher exercising an undue influence; but democratic education is the only long-term safeguard against tyranny.

The enemies of free discussion in education fall into two main categories. There are those who are totalitarian at heart, and believe in education as indoctrination—whether of intellectual and social inferiors who are to serve them, or of fellow members of a self-perpetuating *élite*. And there are those who dare not face discussion because they are afraid of it; they feel that their own ideas, if really tested, could only go down in defeat. But free discussion, if conducted with tact and courtesy, ought not to be inhibited by the totalitarian or the fearful. One could argue that the seminar, of all teaching methods, has its democratic priorities most inescapably right.

Exercise

I

A seminar on Wordsworth's '*She dwelt among th'untrodden ways*', with questions.

> She dwelt among th'untrodden ways
>   Beside the springs of Dove,
> A Maid whom there were none to praise
>   And very few to love.
>
> A Violet by a mossy stone
>   Half-hidden from the Eye!
> —Fair, as a star when only one
>   Is shining in the sky!
>
> She *liv'd* unknown, and few could know
>   When Lucy ceas'd to be;
> But she is in her Grave, and Oh!
>   The difference to me.

This poem was recently discussed at the first session in a

practical criticism course, with about twenty students present. First of all the poem was read aloud; then, under the influence of tea and comfortable armchairs, a desultory conversation about Wordsworth began, full of personal prejudices and half-formed ideas. After a little while the instructor drew in as many as possible of those who had not spoken, and asked them to give a brief account of their feelings about the poem.

The result, for a first meeting, was not unexpected. Only three students said they liked the poem. They were unable to give any detailed reasons, but they talked about its profundity, its 'music', its success in depicting the poet's shock that such a simple person should have died. A vociferous group insisted that the poem was trite, conventional, banal, not much different from 'Twinkle, twinkle, little star'. One girl recalled how she had said all this to a sixth-form teacher, but that in 'A' level she had repeated *his* views rather than her own. The middle-of-the-road students produced the phrase 'mildly pleasing', and went no farther. About half the students found difficulty in breaking the ice.

There are a number of readers who find all the simple poems in *Lyrical Ballads* embarrassing, but this does not explain the response of the seminar. Famous passages from Spenser, Milton, Dryden, Pope, Gray or Tennyson have been offered to first seminars in practical criticism with the same negative results. Many students at school or university do not at first enjoy a large amount of the literature they study, and there is a real danger that they will retreat, when confronted with the challenge to discuss it, into either silence or hypocrisy. The important thing is for them to keep an open mind, to attend to other opinions, and to join in, no matter how tentatively, as soon as they have any personal contribution to make, or any question to ask.

In this seminar on Lucy, the instructor next provided some background information. Wordsworth wrote the poem at

Goslar in 1799. Goslar is in Germany at the foot of the Harz mountains, and Dorothy and William were forced to spend a long, severe winter there, couped up in inadequate lodgings. They could speak little German, had few acquaintances, and the cold made trips into the surrounding countryside impossible. It seems that the peculiar intensity of the Lucy poems, together with their pessimism, is in some degree attributable to this strange, prison-like experience. The students were interested in these details, but their appreciation was not immediately helped.

In the seminar more tea was served, and as the students chatted, two of them noted something odd about the poem. One pointed out that the two images in the middle stanza appear to contradict each other. The beauty of the violet is half-hidden, a secret only discerned by a watchful eye. The star is visible to everyone; in fact attention is attracted to it because it is alone in the sky. Another student asked what 'none to praise And very few to love' was supposed to mean. The instructor then took the class through the poem line by line trying to show that it is not as simple as it looks.

In the first line, 'untrodden ways' is almost a contradiction. The image of a 'way', like a road or a beaten-down path, has to co-exist with an image of a place where people do not tread. The resulting confusion in one's mind is a very typical response to Wordsworth's best poetry. 'Untrodden' suggests undespoiled, innocent, simple; 'ways' reminds us of a way of life, and hints at mysterious places inhabited only by rare souls. The phrase is powerfully evocative, suggesting that Lucy dwells in mysterious communion with Nature. The poem is a little like a fairy-tale, and the simple rhythms and rhyme scheme enforce this effect. The idea that she *dwells* in a *way* is unusual, and is reminiscent of the Bible. Lucy appears to live perpetually moving in mysterious, innocent ways; but perhaps it is wrong to interpret this line too precisely. The image of 'untrodden ways' is unlocalised, and evokes a state of mind.

No scholar has managed to work out which river Dove is meant in the second line. There are rivers of this name in Derbyshire, Yorkshire and Westmorland. This uncertainty suits the poem, for clearly Wordsworth chose the name for his rhyme and for its symbol: 'the springs of Dove' suggests that Lucy haunts the very sources of peace. The plural 'springs', together with 'ways', makes one feel that Lucy does not live in one place, but is part of a landscape. In the third and fourth lines an apparently simple statement again becomes mysterious. It is easy to offer some rational explanation for these lines; perhaps she was loved by the few people in her family, and because they lived alone, never praised by the outside world; but this interpretation does not do justice to the structure of the statement. Usually when we say that no one did some action and very few did another, we imply that the action no one accomplished is superior to that managed by the very few: 'no one scored full marks and very few got more than 70 per cent.' In these lines, therefore, though it is clearly better 'to love' than 'to praise', the structure of the statement suggests the exact opposite. One result is that 'none to praise' takes on added meaning. The solitude of Lucy is emphasised, her withdrawal from the ordinary world, and the few that love are placed at a distance, perhaps in an inferior position.

In the class it was agreed that it is difficult to analyse the exact effect of these mysterious contradictions. The structure of the poem is based upon them. The apparent contradiction in 'untrodden ways' is paralleled by the opposition between the half-hidden violet and the fair star shining by itself in the sky. The peculiarity of 'none to praise And very few to love' occurs again in the first two lines of the final stanza. The opposition of the violet and the star suggests two schemes of values. Lucy's simplicity is hidden to the ordinary world, but in the heavens she is the only star. In the first lines of the concluding stanza, the structure of the sentence gives an added meaning to 'She *liv'd* unknown'. This evokes the feeling that Lucy lived in *the* un-known, at one with the secret of the universe.

Many of the students found the last two lines bathetic. In fact their relation to the rest of the poem is not so simple as it appears on a first reading. The effect of the description of Lucy is to take her out of this world into a mysterious union with Nature, the unknown, the land of fairy; yet she is in her grave, and this simple statement offers no consoling suggestion that she has returned to Nature or to God. The first draft of the poem was sent from Goslar in a letter to Coleridge. Soon afterwards in another letter Wordsworth included the poem Coleridge called a sublime epitaph:[1]

> A slumber did my spirit seal,
>   I had no human fears:
> She seem'd a thing that could not feel
>   The touch of earthly years.
>
> No motion has she now, no force;
>   She neither hears nor sees,
> Roll'd round in earth's diurnal course
>   With rocks and stones and trees!

In this poem there is a definite contrast between the dream-like first stanza, with its promise that Lucy will never die, and the harsh reality of death. 'She dwelt among th'untrodden ways' ends in a similar way. The poem has made us aware of the mystery of Lucy's personality, her almost divine simplicity. Yet she is dead, and in the last line it is as if a whole area of Wordsworth's consciousness had been taken from him.

And so the seminar concluded, and at least the students went away arguing about the poem.

Questions

1. Discuss honestly your feelings about the poem both before

[1] See Mary Moorman's *William Wordsworth. A Biography. The Early Years. 1770–1803* for the full biographical details.

and after you read the commentary. Do you feel that the interpretation offers unnecessary subtleties? Did the commentary help you to enjoy the poem?

2. List the ambiguities that exist in the poem. Consider, in particular, the curious ambiguities of Wordsworth's *praise*. Suppose that the third and fourth lines of Stanza 1 were presented to you out of context. Might you not think that the 'Maid' was a delinquent or a criminal, and that the poet simply meant that she was worthless and unlovable? Consider, again, the effect of the third and fourth lines of Stanza 2, if taken out of context. Would this not seem insulting if paraphrased unkindly? —'fair as a star in the sky, as long as there is no other star with which to compare it'?

Why do you imagine that these—and other—ambiguities exist in the poem? Are they a sign of structural weakness? Or does Wordsworth deliberately court them, as part of his total effect?

3. Discuss in detail, or write a fuller analysis of, 'A Slumber did my Spirit Seal'.

4. Why do you imagine that many readers *think* they have understood these two poems fully, when in fact they have not? How does one get the impression that they are 'simple'?

Exercise

2

A Seminar on R. S. Thomas' '*Here*', with questions.

The following notes were taken at a seminar of first-year undergraduates in their third term at the University of East Anglia. The students had read the poem in advance, and probably discussed it informally among themselves. The class lasted for one and a half hours, and included twenty members—rather a large number for a discussion of this kind. Everybody contributed something, and the instructor (one of ourselves) had little to do but take notes.

We suggest that you spend some time considering the poem before looking at the following account—which reflects an interplay of minds at work and not, of course, an organised analysis. You are then asked to consider the questions at the end.

Here

I am a man now.
Pass your hand over my brow,
You can feel the place where the brains grow.

I am like a tree,
From my top boughs I can see
The footprints that led up to me.

There is blood in my veins
That has run clear of the stain
Contracted in so many loins.

Why, then, are my hands red
With the blood of so many dead?
Is this where I was misled?

Why are my hands this way
That they will not do as I say?
Does no God hear when I pray?

I have nowhere to go.
The swift satellites show
The clock of my whole being is slow.

It is too late to start
For destinations not of the heart.
I must stay here with my hurt.

'What is the poem about?'

'It's a poem about a person looking at himself.'

'It's a very simple poem, very childlike. The images are so basic; "I am like a tree" and so on.'

'Yes: a bit Wordsworthian.'

'Not really like Wordsworth, though.'

'No: the tone's different. But it is childlike without being childish, Wordsworthian in that sense.'

'But not mystical like Wordsworth. You feel the poet has his feet on the ground. It is full of strong common sense. Religious in a way, but not mystical.'

'I'm not so sure about this. To me, it's a bit sinister. Isn't it like *Frankenstein*? To me, it's like the monster coming alive, and becoming aware of himself, and realising his evil. He's doomed and terribly conscious of it. You feel sorry for him.'

'That's a bit far-fetched, isn't it? I read it more like Modern Man in a mechanical age, seeing himself as ruined. It's against machines, like Ruskin and Lawrence . . .' ('and Carlyle,' 'and Morris,' 'and Leavis,' 'and Blake' . . ., etc.: general hubbub).

. . . 'I feel the poet hates machines. The satellites must be the sputniks, perhaps the poet wrote it when the first ones went up, and he feels that he is left behind by the modern world,' . . .

. . .'Yes, but it's the modern world he's judging, not himself. He feels that he represents the true human tradition, but he's lost. The poem says: Be human. Don't make things. Be human. But it also says, we can't be human any more. We've lost.'

'I agree that all this is in the poem, but basically I still think it is just one man looking at himself. And I *mean* one man. I think there's only one man it could be.'

'Who?'

'Christ. Isn't this a poem about Christ?'

(Pause, while everyone reads through the poem again.)

'It could be, I suppose.'

'But why *only* Christ?'

'I think the clue is in stanza 3:

There is blood in my veins
That has run clear of the stain
Contracted in so many loins.

No ordinary man could say this. Only one man is sinless—traditionally—and that is Christ. The speaker is thinking of the man whose blood is uniquely sinless but who has the burden of the world's sin on him.'

'But why stanza 4 then? Christ didn't kill anyone.'

'Yes, but that is just the point. He is sacrificed for the sins of others. He takes our blood on him.'

'Wait a minute: if this *is* Christ, then the poem must be about one particular moment. It is Christ on the Cross. And the imagery in stanzas 4 to 7 is not figurative but literal. His hands won't move because they are nailed. They are red with his own blood, which is also the blood of all human killing.'

'But stanza 5 doesn't fit. How could Christ say this?'

'But that fits in too. If this *is* Christ on the cross, it must be one particular moment, the moment of doubt: "My God, my God, why hast Thou forsaken me?" The sixth stanza would refer to the darkness over the face of the earth (not to the sputniks), and the last stanza would be the moment when Christ is finally alienated from God, but accepts his destiny.'

'If this is true, then stanza 1 becomes extremely rich. The first line, "I am a man now" becomes Christ's realisation that he is a real man and no longer God: the physical reality of the brains is the reality of his flesh, *and* of mortality. But there is another level as well. He is also a man through suffering; the sense in which you can only really *be* a man when you have come face to face with defeat and death. Like Milton's Samson.'

'The image of the tree would certainly fit. The tree of sin in Eden which caused Christ's suffering. And the footprints would be the genealogical line from Adam and Eve to Christ, a real set of "footprints" '. . .

'Yes: original sin.'

'And the tree of the crucifixion. Wasn't that supposed to be on a tree?'

'But why "misled" in line 4?'

(Pause.)

'Well . . . couldn't that be the nature of the doubt? Perhaps he feels that he should have followed the Messianic path, and not let himself be crucified. This might be part of the temptation.'

'Might it be that he sees his own blood on the heads of his killers?—or foresees the blood to be shed in his Name?—and wonders if it was worth while after all?'

'This would fit with the mood at the end. The choice must be followed out because there is no longer any option. And the title "Here" is the "here" of the last line—the moment of choice, which the poem is about.'

'This is all very well, but I'm not at all convinced. You've made everything fit. . . .'

'Not made, it *does* fit.'

'But you've been reading in . . .'

'Not reading *in*, just reading. The words are all there' . . . (complete hubbub for a minute or two).

'No, but listen: when I first read this, I didn't think of Christ. Most modern readers wouldn't, would they? I agree it fits, but there is another interpretation'. . . .

'I think we were on the right lines till someone mentioned Christ, and that confused things'. . . .

'Yes, that's what I think' . . . (some agreement; but some disagreement too).

'Well, let's start again on another assumption. This is a man, a real man: after all, it doesn't sound like Christ. "Does no God hear when I pray" is definitely human, to my way of thinking. In my view, this is a real man becoming aware of himself as a man rather than as something else.'

'What else?'

'Well . . . a child. This is the moment when a man realises he is no longer a child. He sees that he has to live, and that living is suffering. Like that John Wain poem we discussed.'[1]

'I'm not sure. I agree basically, but where does the second verse fit in?'

'That's the man fully grown, looking back at his own past: the child's experience leading, like footprints, up to the man.'

'The tree would fit as an image of growth; and the blood would be the adult's awareness of guilt, the end of innocence.'

'Nearly right, but I've a better idea. Isn't this man realising that he isn't an *animal*?'

'What do you mean: the first man historically, whoever he was? Or any man? One of us?'

'The second—or either. It could be both. I don't think that matters. There *is* a point where one sees that one is not like other animals. Perhaps not all at once, like this—but all poets put things intensely.'

'Let's see how to read the poem like this.'

'All right: line 1. This is the realisation that man has come of age. His brains separate him from the animals and they are really "there": you can feel the place where they grow.'

'But his brains are physical, and they link him to the animal by an evolutionary chain.'

'The tree is the whole chain of evolution, and from the top— the brains are at the top—you can at last *see* the process. Because you have a brain, you cease to be just part of a process, and become aware of cause and effect, and of your own part. That's what a brain means.'

'But how do you fit stanza 3 with this?'

'Easily. The animals live by preying on one another, the battle of life' . . .

('Nature-red-in-tooth-and-claw: Tennyson') . . .

. . . 'the survival of the fittest' . . .

[1] 'Time Was' from *Weep Before God.*

. . . 'Yes: and man feels that he is superior to this, because of his brain.' . . .

. . .'but then is disillusioned. He finds that despite his superior intellect, he is still involved in bloodshed and murder. And he wonders why. Why can't he do as he says? This is the whole business of original sin, the Pauline thing, "The good that I would I do not, the evil that I would not, that I do" . . .'

. . . 'And he wonders why God doesn't help.'

'Then perhaps the satellites *are* the sputniks, and "here" is our present historical moment, and the poet feels that the whole modern world has taken a wrong turning, from which there's no escape.'

'I'm interested in the opposition between "head" and "heart". At first the speaker feels his brains, and thinks that these should make him superior to the brutes, but discovers that they appear not to. So then he turns to the heart. It is too late for the head to help, so one turns to the heart. A last refuge.'

'The line "Is this where I was misled?" fits. If man had followed the heart in the first place, he would have fulfilled his superiority, and the drift to despair would have been averted.'

'So the imagery in stanzas 4 to 7 *is* figurative after all—the poet is saying that we have a kind of collective guilt.'

'What I feel is that the poet is really on the side of the body, despite all this. The poem is full of images with a strong physical sense, and with images of growth—"brains grow", "tree", "top bough", "veins", "loins", "heart". You feel that there is a kind of strength in this—a strength tugging against the pessimism of the thought.'

'I agree. "Satellites" and "clock" are mechanical, and they are bad: you feel this against the strength of the organic images.'

'Well,' 'No,' 'I don't agree,' (etc.) . . .

. . . 'I think that's wrong. Of course if you take "satellites" as sputniks it *could* be like that. But I think "The clock of my whole being" is a natural clock, not a mechanical one—the rhythm of

41

life as it was in the past. And "swift satellites" may be just the speeding up of time, the sense that events are moving too quickly for us, that we're losing control.'

'Something we haven't discussed yet is the poem's structure. The organisation into triplets is most effective—four stanzas with full rhyme, the other three (stanzas 1, 3 and 7) with half-rhyme. It begins and ends with half-rhyme, and that is important, isn't it? You feel a kind of stoicism in it, an acceptance of doubt and incompleteness. Then it looks to me as though there is an underlying logical structure: stanzas 1 to 3 thesis, stanzas 4 to 6 antithesis, stanza 7 synthesis. First you have the speaker's realisation of his manhood, with his reasons for feeling superior to the stages leading up to him—the top of the tree. Then you have his further realisation of his lack of real superiority, conveyed in these terribly bare, terribly unanswerable questions. And finally the conclusion: the brains have seemed to offer superiority, but have failed. So now he turns to the heart. But the situation is desperate.'

'True: but don't you see, this logical framework would still work if you thought the speaker was Christ? The precise meaning would be slightly different, but the process of argument could be the same. And I still think that stanza 3 would fit in better with this.'

'To my mind, the fact that we're not sure of the speaker's identity is part of the poem's success. At first I wasn't sure, but now the poem makes such an impact . . .'

'. . . Yes, you feel its force and energy: this is the place to start from. . . .'

'. . . Agreed: we wouldn't bother with it if it didn't carry its own—well, authority. . . .'

'. . . There's something elemental about it. . . .'

'. . . At first, I thought it so simple that there was nothing to say: but that was wrong. . . .'

'. . . The real secret is the language: the words are so powerfully alive here: mostly monosyllables, and very basic words like "man", "brains", "loins", "blood", but brought alive here with a kind of urgency; this is what a really good poem does.'

'Yes, but the rhythm helps. There's no metre—or rather no consistent metre—but you can feel the poet's strength and integrity in the rhythms.'

'Yes: but to get back to this matter of the speaker's identity. Its not exactly ambivalence, is it? It's something odder than that. The poem has two *total* meanings, each of which fits completely, but each of which demands different interpretations throughout. The first line, for instance. If this is an ordinary man speaking, he means: "I am a man now, and no longer an animal: something more than an animal." But if this is Christ, he means "I am a man now, and no longer God: something less than God, but also a *real* man". And all the way through, each stanza means something different. If the speaker is Christ, the imagery is mainly literal, with figurative overtones. If it is an ordinary man speaking, the imagery is figurative, but powerful because of its physical concreteness.'

'But do you think the poet attempted this? Or is it a sort of accident?'

'I think he meant it.'

'I'm not sure about that.'

'If he didn't mean it, there's an odd coincidence here.'

'If he *did* mean it, then the poem's a triumph, isn't it? Now that I've got used to it, the two meanings seem to support one another. One can hold them together even though the shades of interpretation differ. I get the picture now of modern man, troubled by the world he lives in, but with Christ on the cross in the background, as a reminder that this isn't only modern, and that man's suffering is entirely related to Christ's. This is why the poem doesn't feel wholly pessimistic, despite what it says.'

'You mean that our modern experience is linked to Christ's?'

'Yes.'

'That's why the two interpretations don't strain against one another. They are linked in experience and the same images are appropriate to each.'

'I think this is a poem on two levels, like much of Eliot's poetry, and that the poet intended it to be.'

'If the poet didn't intend it, then the effect is even more remarkable.'

'Perhaps it is because he is a Christian poet? He would be used to associating human suffering with Christ, and his sense of despair and tragedy would naturally gather up religious associations.'

'To my mind, the second meaning we talked about is the basic one; man realising his evolutionary position. And the Christian meanings are secondary—a kind of powerful overtone through-out, which the poet might or might not have been conscious of.',

'I agree. I think our discussion was the wrong way round because the idea of Christ was brought in too early. . . .'

'. . . I brought it in because I *felt* it. . . .'

'But I agree it is there.'

'I still think there is a lot more to be said about this poem. . . .'

At this point, time ran out. The discussion was one of a series in a course on 'Poetry since 1945'. When R. S. Thomas came to read his poems a few days later, he was asked about '*Here*' by several students. Predictably, he refused to be specific, and reminded us that a poet says all he can say in the poem itself: a paraphrase is the last thing he can be expected to give. But he did add that a poem is naturally enriched if its meaning is 'multivalent'.

Questions

1. One early speaker says: 'To me, it's a bit sinister. Isn't it like *Frankenstein*?' This suggestion is called 'far-fetched'. Do you agree?

2. 'The poem says: Be human. Don't make things. Be

human'. Do you think that the word 'make' was well chosen by the speaker? Do you agree with him?

3. Of the two main interpretations offered, which seems to you the more central? Do you agree that the poem is capable of both interpretations? If you had been taking part in this discussion, would you have agreed with the idea that *both* interpretations should be held in a reader's mind simultaneously?

4. If the poem is about Christ, then it must be specifically about the moment of doubt on the Cross. Do you think that stanzas 4 and 5 are consistent with this?

5. Would you agree that the theme of man's place in the evolutionary scale is reflected in the poet's choice of imagery?

6. Give your own comments on the following propositions, relating them, of course, to their context in the discussion:

(a) 'Then perhaps the satellites *are* sputniks, and "here" is our present historical moment, and the poet feels that the whole modern world has taken a wrong turning from which there is no escape.'

(b) 'What I feel is that the poet is really on the side of the body' . . .

(c) 'Then it looks to me as though there is an underlying logical structure: stanzas 1 to 3 thesis, stanzas 4 to 6 antithesis, stanza 7 synthesis.'

7. Consider the precise implications of:

(a) 'feel' (line 3)

(b) 'led up to' (line 6)

(c) 'misled' (line 12)

(d) 'swift satellites' (line 17)

(e) 'here' (line 21)

Exercise

3

A seminar on Philip Larkin's *'Lines on a Young Lady's Photograph Album'*, with questions.

At last you yielded up the album, which,
Once open, sent me distracted. All your ages
Matt and glossy on the thick black pages!
Too much confectionery, too rich:
I choke on such nutritious images.

My swivel eye hungers from pose to pose—
In pigtails, clutching a reluctant cat;
Or furred yourself, a sweet girl-graduate;
Or lifting a heavy-headed rose
Beneath a trellis, or in a trilby hat

(Faintly disturbing, that, in several ways)—
From every side you strike at my control,
Not least through these disquieting chaps who loll
At ease about your earlier days:
Not quite your class, I'd say, dear, on the whole.

But o, photography! as no art is,
Faithful and disappointing! that records
Dull days as dull, and hold-it smiles as frauds,
And will not censor blemishes
Like washing-lines, and Hall's Distemper boards,

But shows the cat as disinclined, and shades
A chin as doubled when it is, what grace
Your candour thus confers upon her face!

How overwhelmingly persuades
That this is a real girl in a real place,

In every sense empirically true!
Or is it just *the past*? Those flowers, that gate,
These misty parks and motors, lacerate
Simply by being over; you
Contract my heart by looking out of date.

Yes, true; but in the end, surely, we cry
Not only at exclusion, but because
It leaves us free to cry. We know *what was*
Won't call on us to justify
Our grief, however hard we yowl across

The gap from eye to page. So I am left
To mourn (without a chance of consequence)
You, balanced on a bike against a fence;
To wonder if you'd spot the theft
Of this one of you bathing; to condense,

In short, a past that no one now can share,
No matter whose your future; calm and dry,
It holds you like a heaven, and you lie
Unvariably lovely there,
Smaller and clearer as the years go by.

You are asked to read and think about the above poem, and then to read the discussion which follows. The discussion is taken from notes on a seminar in which students from several age-groups took part.

You are then asked to answer the questions at the end.

Discussion

'Is there any point in analysing a poem like this? There's no problem about what it means.'

'What does it mean?'

'Well, that's obvious.'

'It depends upon what you mean by "meaning".'

'Isn't that a quibble?'

'No. After all, a poem never does "mean" its paraphrasable content. There is the interaction of this with all kinds of other things—the metre and stanza form, the verbal suggestiveness, the tone. My first impression is that the tone of this poem is very important.'

'I agree. And I'm not sure that the poem's meaning is clear anyway, even in a paraphrasable sense. For instance, is it meant philosophically? If you look at stanzas 7 and 8, you might think the poem was leading up to a general statement about "life". But in the poem as a whole, one senses that these reflections exist for a special purpose, to define very precisely Larkin's feelings about this girl.'

'But wait a minute . . .'

'Wait a minute!' . . .

(Two very strong objections simultaneously.)

'Can I speak first? Well, I'm not sure that the last speaker should have said "Larkin". We don't know if it is the poet himself.'

'It sounds like the poet.'

'I think it's the poet.'

'No, isn't it a *persona*? Not exactly a dramatic monologue, but half way to that? You don't feel the poem is a direct expression of the poet's feelings, however personal it sounds. If you look closely, you see it is a very skilful artefact. The metre is beautifully precise, so is the rhyme scheme, and the speaking voice moves delicately against metre and rhyme, offering the illusion of conversation' . . .

. . .'Yes, a kind of social tone: well, social *and* personal. That is to say, the poet's dialogue with the girl is socially poised, yet it sounds as though he is musing to himself. In stanza 8, for instance, he wonders whether she would "spot the theft" of the photograph of herself bathing. You wouldn't actually say this out loud to the girl would you, even playfully? And the last stanza is very personal and private.'

'This is important, surely. My bewilderment is about just this. Is the poet actually talking to the girl, teasing her as (say) Yeats does in "For Ann Gregory"? Or is he musing by himself on what he did say to her, or might say?'

'Now you bring this forward, I'd say that it's a very lonely poem. The poet doesn't sound to me as though he'd have the courage to speak to the girl at all. It's more like a daydream, things you would like to have said.'

'But the poet admits that: or rather, the whole poem is about a past that didn't happen because the poet didn't propose to her. (Isn't that what it's about?) I think he can talk to the girl well enough socially, but this bantering voice is his defence against talking more seriously. In fact, it may be just because he spoke to her like this in the past that she didn't take him seriously then.'

'I wouldn't take a man seriously who spoke to me like this.' (Laughter.)

'In other words, he's the sort of man who doesn't take opportunities, though I'm not sure that "courage" has anything to do with it. Probably he just doesn't take himself seriously, it's a form of modesty or self-mistrust.'

'Surely the present situation is his own choice? If you look at his other poems, "No Road", "Dockery and Son", oh lots of others, you'll see that he chose not to get married. He feels marriage would have swamped him. But he half regrets this, and considers the future that *might* have been: much stronger and more real than what he actually has.'

'The more poignant the past, the more wraith-like the present?'

'This seems to me to be getting nearer the truth. Isn't he the sort of man who always thinks another future would have been better? In "Maiden Names", it works the other way round. A woman who has married feels that her maiden self is somehow dead and unfulfilled.'

' "Love Songs in Age" would support this. Love is made to sound nothing but a cheat.'

'May I say that I object to the way this discussion is going very strongly? What you forget is firstly that these are poems, and not pieces of autobiography; and secondly, that they deal with moments of intense awareness, not with statements about "life". That "Maiden Names" poem, for instance, is almost eerily right. That is exactly how you do feel when coming suddenly on an old school report, yellow with age, and bearing a name you no longer have. And "Love Songs in Age" is beautifully tender. How can you say that "Love is made to sound nothing but a cheat"?'

'That is all very well, but there are so many of Larkin's poems with this same theme and general feeling. They must relate to the poet's own temperament?—though not directly, like auto-biography, I agree.'

'Larkin always seems to feel the poignancy, the nostalgia in life. There is that very haunting moment in "Ambulances", when he speaks of "the solving emptiness/That lies just under all we do". I feel the emptiness in this poem as well. The image in the last stanza here is desolating in its awareness.'

'This is exactly what I feel about Larkin's lighter tone, his banter and cynicism; the lighter tone is an attempt to protect himself from too much self-knowledge, too much awareness of emptiness.'

'I'm sorry to be odd man out, but may I say again that I think this discussion has got completely on the wrong track? You are all taking a much too simple view. Can I get back for a minute to my earlier suggestion about a *persona*? The fact to remember is that this is not a spontaneous meditation, even though the poet's art is to make it sound like one. It is a highly wrought poem, with its own distinctive structure. You'll notice that it begins on a note of light-hearted banter, then moves gradually towards intellectual honesty, and finally through intellectual honesty to complete emotional seriousness. Those last two stanzas are among the most beautiful in any poem I've ever read. They are profoundly serious, and they are the point to which the whole poem moves. If you think of "Churchgoing", you'll remember that there, too, you have exactly the same kind of progression that I've just described, from initial banter and mockery, through intellectual honesty, to emotional honesty and complete seriousness. In my own experience this particular approach to honesty is very typical not only of Larkin, but of the whole post-war generation to which he belongs. We are terrified of being solemn, but we have to take ourselves seriously sometimes. What one must always remember is that in a poem, this kind of progression doesn't just *happen*. It is part of the poem's plan, so that the aspects we have just been discussing can't possibly be looked on as the poet caught off his guard—a loophole for us to psychoanalyse him, or to find out more about him than he knows himself. He invites us to respond to the flexibilities of tone as well as to the "meaning" (this, incidentally, answers the question this discussion started from): the shifts of tone are planned from the start.'

'Yes,' 'But,' 'Well,' 'This may be true, but' . . . (signs of widespread but uneasy disagreement).

'Look: oughtn't we to look more closely at this poem before we generalise any further? Let us try going through it stanza by stanza, and then we'll see more clearly whether we agree with the last speaker or not.'

'Right. In the first two lines, he gets the girl to give him the album.'

'She's been flirting with him.'

'Not flirting; she's just playful.'

'Of course she wants him to get it.'

'It's unbelievably Victorian, isn't it? Like one of those awful women in Tennyson, "Airy, fairy Lilian" and the rest.'

'Oh no: just feminine.'

'But not modern. There's a kind of artificiality about it all; the title deliberately suggests something Victorian, doesn't it? You feel that they know their whole relationship is safe: part of a game.'

'That seems to me to be borne out by what follows. The poet captures the mood, and teases her.'

'How do you mean?'

'The overstatement. He says he is "distracted", but he certainly doesn't sound it. And the "nutritious images" makes her seem like a box of chocolates.'

'And "My swivel eye hungers from pose to pose" carries on this mood. It is the sort of remark which looks like a joke at your expense but is really more a joke at the other person's.'

'How do you mean?'

'Well, it sounds so cool and collected. So when he says he is "distracted", that he chokes and hungers, there's a built-in anti-climax—as though he's really mocking the idea of passionate love itself, and therefore mocking the lady as someone who might inspire it. Do you see?'

'I disagree. There is nothing malicious about this' . . .

. . . 'I didn't say "malicious" ' . . .

. . . 'It is all rather delicate, in fact. I feel that he does admire the lady, but expresses this through irony because they are both sophisticated people.'

'This reminds me a little of Pope's attitude to Belinda in "The Rape of the Lock": ostensibly overpraising her in order to deflate, but really meaning the flattery as well. . . . The tone's different, of course. Pope uses the conventions of the mock-heroic, where you expect this strategy; this poem is more personal, more conversational. I still think it's the tone of people who like one another but never think of taking one another seriously . . . of marrying, that is.'

'It could be the tone of a man and woman who like one

another, but one of them loves somebody else more, so they retreat into banter.'

'What do you make of the tone of stanza 3? The poet sounds here like an upper-class snob.'

'That's part of the humour, though. He adopts the tone of an upper-class snob to make his point, but you feel that this is the last tone that comes naturally to him. It's a way of turning the joke back on himself again' . . .

. . . 'and keeping the temperature down' . . .

. . . 'like mock-Cockney, you mean?'

'Yes: a private joke.'

'All this business of tone! You're making it impossibly complicated.'

'Not at all. The tone of intimate conversation usually is complicated. It only sounds complicated when you're analysing it as we're doing now.'

'Think of Eliot's "Portrait of a Lady", for instance! The complexity of this is child's play to that.'

'But why analyse it, then?'

'To read the poem properly. To my mind, Larkin is unusually conscious of tone' . . .

. . . 'Aren't we all?' (Laughter.)

. . . 'and he captures these nuances beautifully: it is part of his triumph to make it sound so easy.'

'Stanza 4 strikes me as a transition. That "o, photography?" is mocking again, as though he *is* using mock-heroic conventions. But then it gets more serious: we sense that the fidelity of a photograph, which betrays most things, makes the girl more lovely.'

'I'm struck by the accuracy of observation. That line "clutching a reluctant cat" is exactly right, this is just how nine out of ten cats do look in photographs' . . .

. . . 'outraged, because made to do something they don't want.'

'The "Hall's Distemper boards" are just right too.'

'Then comes what seems to be the philosophical part, "In every sense empirically true!" I can't feel that most girls would be thrilled by that. (Laughter.) But one can see that he is really thinking about the status of the photograph. What really moves him in it? Is it just the realism of detail which he has commented on, proving that the girl is beautiful quite apart from his feelings for her, as a matter of *fact*? Or is it more subjective and emotional, his response to "*the past*"? This is clearly the heart of the poem. It is somewhat like Ted Hughes looking at the photograph of six young men who have been killed in the war,[1] and being torn between several kinds of reality' . . .

'Less strong than Ted Hughes, surely!'

'A different sort of strength. Ted Hughes is concerned with heroism, Philip Larkin with nostalgia.'

'Nostalgia isn't strong, anyway.'

'Why not? That's a stock-response. All sensitive people feel nostalgia.'

'Yes, but he's luxuriating in it.'

'No: just defining it. He makes it as precisely real as he does the "reluctant cat". And to make an emotion real in this way is rare.'

'He does it through the concrete imagery in stanza 6, and above all by the last line. This is exactly what you do feel when looking at (say) a photograph of your mother in 1930 clothes. Or better still, your grandmother.'

'Exactly! But a grandmother's not exactly a girl friend, is she?'

'No, not fair! Or at least . . . well, I don't think it is. Though perhaps if he'd married the girl, or been the marrying type, he would be more light-hearted than this.'

'The next two stanzas give the game away. He can't bear responsibility.'

'*Not* "give the game away". Why do you keep on talking as

[1] For this poem and our analysis, see pages 88-100.

though you were catching him out? They are an extraordinarily exact piece of emotional honesty.'

'I didn't mean "catch him out" exactly. But he admits, himself, to a fault. The whole meaning is that this kind of nostalgia is too easy. We can have a good cry "without a chance of consequence". Surely the poet is reflecting, though he doesn't say this absolutely explicitly, on his own state of mind? The state of mind which has probably prevented him from marrying in the past.'

'Where do you find that in the poem?'

'The whole attitude.'

'I'm not so sure. Isn't the force of this part of the poem that the poet universalises his feelings? He talks about "us"—"our grief", "we yowl" and so on. He means that this is true of all of us. The particular incident becomes a sort of parable.'

'But does it? I think this attitude is only true of some of us. The attempt to universalise is merely the poet's way of evading a personal judgment.'

'Yet there is a personal judgment here, and a very savage one, I'd have thought. Look at the poet's situation! His love for the girl, the basis for this degree of intimacy, is a mere game. He simply hints it, by suggesting jealousy of the young men photographed with her in her earlier life, and even the hints are self-mocking. And now, all he has to look forward to is having one of the photographs of her, bathing, if he can take it without her finding out! Compare this with the satisfaction of being married to her, and isn't it . . . twilight? He doesn't drive the point home, but it seems pitiful.'

'Yet the end is very beautiful. It really does seem universal—a tragic note, to do with all of us, whether we are temperamentally like the poet or not.'

'The theme of transience is very romantic, certainly' . . .

'We should balance the nostalgia against the precision of style.'

'It is just because the poet knows all that we've talked about that the poem's so good.'

'Well, at least it's a very beautiful poem' . . .

. . . 'metrically beautiful' . . .

. . . 'beautifully precise' . . .

. . . 'whatever one thinks of the poet's attitude' . . .

. . . 'if it *is* the poet.'

Questions

1. Are there any views expressed in this dialogue with which you strongly agree or disagree? If so, elaborate them, with close reference to the poem.

2. Do any statements in this dialogue strike you as vague, or ambiguous? Are there any statements which seem to you insensitive?

3. The participants in the dialogue disagree about whether the speaker of the poem is the poet personally, or some *persona* or figure in a dramatic monologue. What do you think? Is there enough evidence for a clear decision?

4. There seems to be a general assumption among the participants that the speaker of the poem loved the girl in the past and missed (or refused) an opportunity to propose to her. Do you see any strong evidence of this?

5. Do you think that the speaker of the poem tries to make his readers identify themselves with him? If so, how is this done? Do you think it is successful?

6. Consider the *exact* force in the poem of the following phrases (none of which is mentioned in the dialogue):

  (i) 'A heavy-headed rose' (stanza 2, line 4).

  (ii) 'At ease' (stanza 3, line 4).

  (iii) 'confers upon' (stanza 5, line 3).

  (iv) 'The gap from eye to page' (stanza 8, line 1).

  (v) 'like a heaven' (stanza 9, line 3).

  (vi) 'Unvariably lovely' (stanza 9, line 4).

7. Explain as precisely as you can the effect that the following lines have on you:

> . . . So I am left
> To mourn (without a chance of consequence)
> You, balanced on a bike against a fence . . .

8. Develop any reaction of your own to this poem which is not touched upon in the dialogue.

9. If you were looking for someone to read this aloud as part of a Poetry Reading, what kind of voice and mannerisms would you think most appropriate?

10. If you had to organise the material in the dialogue for a formal analysis, how would you set about it?

Exercise
4

An analysis of Donne's '*A Nocturnall Upon S. Lucies Day*', with questions.

1   Tis the yeares midnight, and it is the dayes,
      Lucies, who scarce seaven houres herself unmaskes,
        The Sunne is spent, and now his flasks
        Send forth light squibs, no constant rayes;
5   The worlds whole sap is sunke:
      The generall balme th' hydroptique earth hath drunk,
      Whither, as to the beds-feet, life is shrunke,
      Dead and enterr'd; yet all these seeme to laugh,
      Compar'd with mee, who am their Epitaph.

10   Study me then, you who shall lovers bee
      At the next world, that is, at the next Spring:
        For I am every dead thing,

In whom love wrought new Alchimie.
   For his art did expresse
15 A quintessence even from nothingnesse,
From dull privations, and leane emptinesse:
He ruin'd mee, and I am re-begot
Of absence, darknesse, death; things which are not.

All others, from all things, draw all that's good,
20 Life, soule, forme, spirit, whence they beeing have;
   I, by loves limbecke, am the grave
   Of all, that's nothing. Oft a flood
    Have wee two wept, and so
Drownd the whole world, us two; oft did we grow
25 To be two Chaosses, when we did show
Care to ought else; and often absences
Withdrew our soules, and made us carcasses.

But I am by her death, (which word wrongs her)
Of the first nothing, the Elixer grown;
30   Were I a man, that I were one,
   I needs must know; I should preferre,
    If I were any beast,
Some ends, some means; Yea plants, yea stones detest,
And love; All, all some properties invest;
35 If I an ordinary nothing were,
As shadow, a light, and body must be here.

But I am None; nor will my Sunne renew.
You lovers, for whose sake, the lesser Sunne
   At this time to the Goat is runne
40   To fetch new lust, and give it you,
    Enjoy your summer all;
Since shee enjoyes her long nights festivall,
Let mee prepare towards her, and let mee call
This houre her Vigill, and her Eve, since this
45 Both the yeares, and the dayes deep midnight is.

In his famous essay, 'The Metaphysical Poets', T. S. Eliot argued that poets such as Donne found 'the verbal equivalent for states of mind and feeling'. In Donne's verse there is a unity of reason and emotion, which makes it superior to much that was written in the succeeding centuries. These definitions have been much discussed, and given different meanings by different critics. In part Eliot was comparing the self-indulgence in emotion of some Romantic poets, such as Shelley, with the intelligent exploration of experience that we find in Donne. Very often when we are profoundly affected by joy or grief, we do not lose ourselves in a flood of feeling, but become very self-conscious. We are intellectually aware of what we are feeling, almost mentally surprised by the depth of our emotion. Our brains are in an unusual state of activity, contemplating the reality of what is happening. This type of self-consciousnesf often does not calm down the emotions, but makes us aware os the precise quality of the experience.

In order to express such relationships between reason and emotion, Donne developed the unusual argumentative structure of his poems. In a poem such as 'The Sunne Rising' he argues, with an appearance of logic, that his love is the world, and that therefore the sun need not waste its time shining on the earth, but may take life easy, confining its attentions to his bedroom. To some readers this kind of pseudo-argument seems too extravagant, but particularly since the publication of Eliot's essay, many critics have argued that this wit is a method of conveying profound individual experiences. The poems are written with a dramatic sense of urgency, expressed in the rhythms of speech, and in a concentrated language with considerable emotional implications; we are impressed with the power of Donne's feeling. At the same time the play of wit and the pseudo-logical structure give an impression that Donne is thinking about his experiences, considering their implications. In her Introduction to her Penguin edition of *The Metaphysical Poets*, Helen Gardner writes:

A conceit is a comparison whose ingenuity is more striking than its justness, or, at least, is more immediately striking. . . . In a metaphysical poem the conceits are instruments of definition in an argument or instruments to persuade. The poem has something to say which the conceit explicates or something to urge which the conceit helps to forward.

In serious poems, such as 'A Nocturnall Upon S. Lucies Day', the extravagant arguments are a means of expressing fundamental attitudes towards love and death.

When studying a Donne poem, we need the assistance of notes and comment on the text. The more we know about the exact meaning of the words, and about the poetic conventions of the period, the more we are able to appreciate the subtleties of Donne's technique. Helen Gardner's collection, mentioned above, provides a fairly useful series of explanatory notes. A more detailed survey is given in H. J. C. Grierson's famous commentaries in his edition of The Poems of John Donne, published by Oxford University Press. St. Lucy's day, 13th December, was traditionally regarded as the shortest day, the Winter Solstice, when the sun entered the sign of the Goat (see the last stanza). In the opening stanza of the Nocturnall, Donne is apparently using this dead season of the year as a means of defining his emotions now his beloved is dead. 'Flasks' refers to the stars, which were thought to store up light from the sun. The description of winter most vividly depicts a state of deprivation. Particularly unusual is the idea of the 'sap' of the world sinking into the earth, of the shrinking of life back under the soil. The rhyming words 'sunke' and 'shrunke' emphasise this movement, and by their brevity and sound suggest the completeness of this process of 'shrinkage'. In particular the lines 'The world's whole sap is sunk', given added importance by its position in the stanza, expresses the hugeness of the change of life that takes place each year. The line strikingly conveys a sense of lifelessness, the despair in which Donne himself is lost. Helen Gardner explains the 'beds-feet' by referring to one of Hippocrates' signs of imminent death, when the sick man 'makes the beds feet where the head should be'. This evokes a sense of fear, and makes more clear the implicit parallel between this winter scene and Donne's own state of mind.

The last two lines of the first stanza begin the main argument of the poem. This picture of decay is inadequate to express Donne's own condition. After presenting 'shrinkage' so forcefully, Donne startles the reader by saying that this scene 'seems to laugh' compared with his state of deprivation. The rest of the poem, until the last stanza, continues this argument. Now his beloved is dead, Donne has become 'nothing', more completely emptied of life than any other thing in the world. Grierson writes in his commentary: 'The poem turns upon the thought of degrees in nothingness'.

In the second stanza Donne offers himself for study by future lovers. The line 'At the next world, that is, at the next Spring' suggests that Donne's winter darkness is perpetual, and that spring will start a new world into which he cannot be born. His state, Grierson explains, was already one of 'dull privations and lean emptiness', and Love reduced it still further, making him once more the non-entity he was before he was created. The effect of this stanza comes from the use of 'new Alchimie', 'art' and 'quintessence' in such an unusual context. These suggest the newness of his condition, his surprise at being transformed into 'things which are not'. The fact that such words, usually associated with perfection and creation, are employed to describe a state of 'non-being' gives a sense of shock, conveying Donne's own amazed horror at the completeness of his loss.

The third stanza indicates that this extravagant comparison of himself to 'nothing' is not merely a fanciful exercise of Donne's intelligence. The first four lines continue the argument of the previous stanza, describing love as an alembic, an apparatus used for refining substances, which in his case has turned him into nothing. But in the fourth line he recalls his past love, and the music and the imagery express the depth of his sadness. His love *was* his life, a creation which fulfilled his true nature; so the absence of this love is death, a denial of his proper identity. Love was for him the world, and absence like Chaos before the Creation. By this extravagant comparison, Donne suggests that knowledge comes only from our experiences, above all from personal relationships. By love we are made and unmade; this for us is creation and chaos, existence and non-existence. This emphasis on experience indicates one reason why Donne's thought has been so in tune with twentieth-century ideas. In his secular poems it is often implied that we know only what we perceive, that we are created as individuals by the experience of loving another person.

The fourth stanza continues this argument. In this world, objects are defined by their attributes and their relations. Grierson explains that 'If I were any beast, I should prefer some ends, some means' refers to the Aristotelian and Scholastic doctrine of the soul:

> The soul of man is rational and self-conscious; of beasts perceptive and moving, therefore able to select ends and means; the vegetative soul of plants selects what it can feed on and rejects what it cannot, and so far detests and loves. Even stones, which have no souls, attract and repel.

In the world things define themselves by their relationships, just as a shadow only exists by means of light and body. Donne's identity was defined by his relationship with the woman, and the quality of their love. Now this has gone, he is nothing.

These meanings are summed up in the last stanza in simple, effective language: 'But I am None; nor will my Sunne renew.' His previous attempts to define his nothingness give a new force to this conventional description of his beloved as the 'Sunne'. We have seen how she created his existence, as the sun gives life to Nature. In this last stanza a new rhythm emerges. The short words in the first line slow down the movement, and the iambic beat is more strongly emphasised. Instead of the disturbed rhetorical tones of much of the previous stanzas, we have a more controlled, ritualistic effect. The last four lines, in particular, possess a dignified, solemn music. At first the meaning of the last four lines seems almost a contradiction of what has gone before. In the previous stanzas the extravagant comparisons of himself to an 'elixir' of the first nothing convey a despair which is close to suicide. Now he talks in an almost religious manner about preparations for death. The image of the 'festivall' imparts a feeling of celebration to the woman's death, as if she is a saint. The images of darkness no longer suggest only deprivation. The effect of 'her long nights festivall' and 'the dayes deep midnight' is very different from the feeling of shrinkage conveyed in the first stanza. The darkness hides a mystery more profound than the experiences of ordinary human lovers. Instead of losing himself in despair, Donne accepts his suffering with stoicism, and prepares himself for a Vigil.

In fact this almost mystical conclusion is most appropriate for the poem. All the conceits about his state of nothingness, the desperate attempts to find a language for his misery, prove the value of what he created through love. Although he says he is nothing, the extremes to which his argument is taken prove how much his identity is defined by his past. The extravagant wit shows that the love has deep effects in the present. In the penultimate stanza the parenthesis after death—'which word wrongs her'—suggests that for him she is still a present reality. And so at the end he turns to the belief that her identity could never be extinguished. He concludes in the language of religious meditation, by his tone of reverence once more attesting to the supreme value of his love.

Questions

1. What do you understand by the terms 'metaphysical wit' and 'metaphysical conceits'? Do you think that the 'conceits' in this poem can be regarded, despite their extravagance, as 'instruments of definition in an argument or instruments to persuade'? Consider, in particular, Grierson's remark that 'The poem turns upon the thought of degrees in nothingness'. Do you agree that Donne uses the apparent nonsense of this idea to convey true emotional experience?

2. Donne repeatedly refers in this poem to *older* scientific—or pseudo-scientific—ideas: to alchemy, astrology, Aristotelian and scholastic ideas of 'some ends, some means', the super-stitious view of death-beds in stanza 1. Why do you think that he chose modes of thought which 'the new philosophy' (as he said elsewhere) had called 'in doubt'?

3. 'He concludes in the language of religious meditation, by his tone of reverence once more attesting to the supreme value of his love.' Do you agree? Analyse more closely than the authors have done the imagery and tone of the last stanza.

4. Consider the precise implications of:

    (*a*) 'unmaskes' (line 2)
    (*b*) 'generall balme' (line 6)
    (*c*) 'seeme to laugh' (line 8)
    (*d*) 'next world' (line 11)
    (*e*) 'He ruin'd mee, and I am re-begot
        Of absence, darknesse, death; things which are not.'
        (lines 17 and 18)
    (*f*) 'the whole world, us two' (line 24)
    (*g*) 'Withdrew' (line 27)
    (*h*) 'Were' (line 30)
    (*i*) 'properties' (line 34)
    (*j*) 'None' (line 37)
    (*k*) 'the lesser Sunne' (line 38)
    (*l*) 'enjoyes' (line 42)

5. Read T. S. Eliot's essay 'The Metaphysical Poets' (in his *Selected Essays*). What do you find that this adds to your understanding of this poem?

6. Write an analysis of any one other poem by Donne where techniques similar to those in this poem are used.

Exercise
5

An analysis of Blake's '*The Little Black Boy*', with questions.

My mother bore me in the southern wild,
And I am black, but O! my soul is white;
White as an angel is the English child,
But I am black, as if bereav'd of light.

My mother taught me underneath a tree,
And sitting down before the heat of day
She took me on her lap and kissèd me,
And pointing to the east, began to say:

'Look on the rising sun! there God does live,
And gives His light, and gives His heat away;
And flowers and trees and beasts and men receive
Comfort in morning, joy in the noon day.

'And we are put on earth a little space,
That we may learn to bear the beams of love;
And these black bodies and this sun-burnt face
Is but a cloud, and like a shady grove;

'For when our souls have learn'd the heat to bear,
The cloud will vanish: we shall hear His voice,
Saying: "Come out from the grove, My love and care,
And round My golden tent like lambs rejoice." '

Thus did my mother say, and kissèd me.
And thus I say to little English boy:
When I from black and he from white cloud free
And round the tent of God like lambs we joy,

I'll shade him from the heat, till he can bear
To lean in joy upon our Father's knee;
And then I'll stand and stroke his silver hair,
And be like him, and he will then love me.

A deceptively simple poem: we have heard it dismissed as
trivial. Blake, more than any poet, might remind us that Aquinas
wrote a treatise on the Simplicity of God, and that 'simplicity'
in its sense of wholeness, integrity, unity, has always been one
of the most prized qualities, in art and life.

True simplicity isn't lack of complexity, but an harmonious
ordering of parts: everything, as in this poem, is balanced and
supported. There is no anxiety to be detected: the tone is serene,
the feeling one of unusual health. The little black boy is considering the meaning of his colour. The mood of his meditation is
that of tenderness (flowing from his mother, through him, to
'little English boy'), and acceptance: his colour is God-given
and is, therefore, a blessing, if he can see how. In stanza 1 the
'black/white', 'white/black' see-saw defines the future development. First (the black boy is speaking):

> I am black, but O! my soul is white,

> then:

> White as an angel is the English child
> But . . .

But *what*? Not 'but *his* soul is black'. The black boy's simplicity
and love defeats, effortlessly, this expected antithesis of bitterness, and goes on to explore the situation as it touches himself:

But I am black, *as if* bereav'd of light.

(our italics)

This 'as if' is the problem: and characteristically, the poem turns now to the mother, as remembered by the boy. We are irresistibly reminded, I think, of Madonna and Child; and this evocation is part of Blake's deep intuition that the outsider, the boy despised by others because his colour makes him '*as if* bereav'd of light' is more likely to *be* Christ—and so more likely to have powers of healing—than the comfortable, self-righteous insiders who see him in this way. The mother's lesson is one of outgoing and overflowing tenderness; starting with God, and moving outwards to the world of creatures. 'Look on the rising sun' . . . (a direction typically Blakean): and the lesson follows, not didactically, but as a lived and communicated insight.

> . . . there God does live,
> And gives His light, and gives His heat away . . .

If God gives equally to man and beast, how can the black boy be 'bereaved'? The word 'gives' is alive, here, as it is in few other contexts: purged of any associations remotely connected with bargaining, and including, richly, the creative outpouring, the generosity of love. And the equality of the gift is beautifully underlined in the receiving:

> And flowers and trees and beasts and men receive
> Comfort in morning, joy in the noon day.

The poem's dynamic is in this *equal* giving. A community which includes plants, beasts and men is without respect of persons. The world of 'experience', for Blake, is a world of man-made inequalities—righteous and sinners, patricians and plebeians, white and black, gentile and Jew, master and slave, man and beast. Men set barriers between themselves and others to establish their own superiority and to justify all kinds of cruelties, exploitations, persecutions, enslavements. Love, joy, gladness, acceptance are denied, and put in chains; the spirit of negation is loosed abroad in their place.

It is one of the classic human inequalities—the one connected with colour—that the little black boy considers. And it is through the acceptance of outpoured love as a universal norm that he goes beyond the bitterness of 'experience' to the Blakean vision of innocence. In stanza 4 the poem turns on the pivot of the divine generosity. The 'blackness' which in stanza 1 seemed a deprivation of light is now seen as arising from excess of light. The 'beams of love' have shone more fully on the black boy than on the white; he is sunburnt by exposure to them. And this very exposure gives him something to offer to the white boy: the attitude of mind which can learn to bear the beams of love. The black body, like the white body, also, of the English boy, 'Is but a cloud, and like a shady grove'. When the cloud lifts, black and white will meet in the Father's love. And then the black boy will have his grace to offer: an offering the return for which will be love.

The last two stanzas are the black boy's message to the English boy—love of God, mediated by way of the mother's tender insight. In the penultimate stanza, the image of the cloud suggests the mystery of the body, the imprecision of the senses which will disappear when we are reborn into a new Heaven. And the final two lines of the poem have the beauty peculiar to those rare occasions when cynicism and bitterness are challenged on their home ground and routed by the sheer force of innocence. Miranda's famous outburst in *The Tempest* is one such occasion.

> How beauteous mankind is! O brave new world,
> To have such people in it.

This isn't (need one say?) a joke for the sophisticated at

Miranda's expense; it is an exquisite insight beyond the actions of Alonso and Antonio to what, after the purgation by tempest, they potentially *are*. It is a classic example of innocence going through words which could only, in the world of experience, be profoundly ironic, to the simpler, deeper truth beyond. Similarly, Blake's little black boy. His closing reflection is the very stuff of irony: the words almost challenge a tone of bitter protest to take control.

> And then I'll stand and stroke his silver hair,
> And be like him, and he will then love me.

But the tone isn't bitter or ironic: equally, it isn't naïve or unperceptive. The mood is one of joyful sincerity, and because of this, uniquely healing in its properties. Not only will the black boy be like the white, but the white boy will be like the black. The barriers gone, they will each be able to give to the other—the 'giving' which has been established as the divine heart of things.

True simplicity, we suggested, isn't lack of complexity, but an harmonious ordering of parts. In all of Blake's Songs of Innocence there is a deep awareness that bitterness, separation, negation are hellish things, even if they claim the sanctions of Heaven; and that law and love, rightly understood, are not opposites, but the two different sides of maturity. In a healthy world, 'love' isn't licence, 'law' isn't 'Thou Shalt Not'. Both spring from an experience of mutuality inside a universe ruled over by a God who 'gives His light, and gives His heat away'. And the little black boy, secure in this intuition, has the positive vision which destroys divisions and bitterness, and enables the creatures of God to meet, despite their differences, in the freedom of love.

The style of the poem is wholly at one with the content. The easy, flowing movement of the lines is as far removed from banality as the things they are saying and being. The centralities of the little black boy's innocence are his sincerity, his positive vision, his acceptance of creative love as the final law of things, his awareness of harmony. These qualities are equally to be detected in the style—where translucent, untroubled serenity and limpid clarity consort easily and naturally with a wonderfully alert word usage (in few other contexts do any of these words live so richly, yet unobtrusively, with other words); and a marvellously delicate organisation and progress. Style and content alike offer a hard, burning clarity of lived experience, together with a tone and mood of unaffected ease. No poet but Blake has such authentic simplicity as this. For readers of all types of belief, his poems might still seem a master-key to unlock our prison doors.

Questions

1. Discuss the 'simplicity' of this poem, and consider examples of 'simplicity' in other poems where you find similar effects.

2. Are you satisfied with the definition: 'True simplicity isn't lack of complexity, but an harmonious ordering of parts'? What exactly is meant by 'harmonious ordering of parts'?

3. What is meant by 'health' in the second paragraph of the criticism? Do you think it is proper to call a writer's tone 'healthy', or does this introduce moral ideas irrelevant to art?

4. In the commentary it is suggested that the concluding stanza is not ironic. What would be implied if the tone were ironic? Do you agree that there is no trace of irony here?

5. What additions to the commentary would you like to make?

6. Read Blake's other songs of 'innocence' and 'experience'. Can you say precisely what Blake means by these words? Analyse (or discuss) one of the poems of 'experience'.

Exercise
6

A comparison of Lord Herbert of Cherbury's '*Elegy over a Tomb*' with Thomas Hardy's '*The Shadow on the Stone*', with questions.

Lord Herbert of Cherbury's '*Elegy over a Tomb*'

1   Must I then see, alas! eternal night
      Sitting upon those fairest eyes,
    And closing all those beams, which once did rise
      So radiant and bright,
5   That light and heat in them to us did prove
      Knowledge and Love?

Oh, if you did delight no more to stay
      Upon this low and earthly stage,
But rather chose an endless heritage,
10   Tell us at least, we pray,
Where all the beauties that those ashes ow'd
      Are now bestow'd?

Doth the Sun now his light with yours renew?
      Have Waves the curling of your hair?
15   Did you restore unto the Sky and Air,
      The red, and white, and blew?
Have you vouchsafed to flowers since your death
      That sweetest breath?

Had not Heav'ns Lights else in their houses slept,
20   Or to some private life retir'd?
Must not the Sky and Air have else conspir'd,
      And in their Regions wept?

Must not each flower else the earth could breed
   Have been a weed?

25 But thus enrich'd may we not yield some cause
   Why they themselves lament no more?
That must have changed the course they held before,
   And broke their proper Laws,
Had not your beauties giv'n this second birth
30   To Heaven and Earth?

Tell us, for Oracles must still ascend,
   For those that crave them at your tomb:
Tell us, where are those beauties now become,
   And what they now intend:
35 Tell us, alas, that cannot tell our grief,
   Or hope relief.

Thomas Hardy's '*The Shadow on the Stone*'

1   I went by the Druid stone
   That broods in the garden white and lone,
And I stopped and looked at the shifting shadows
   That at some moments fall thereon
5   From the tree hard by with a rhythmic swing,
   And they shaped in my imagining
To the shade that a well-known head and shoulders
   Threw there when she was gardening.

   I thought her behind my back,
10   Yea, her I long had learned to lack,
And I said: 'I am sure you are standing behind me,
   Though how do you get into this old track?'
   And there was no sound but the fall of a leaf
   As a sad response; and to keep down grief
15 I would not turn my head to discover
   That there was nothing in my belief.

Yet I wanted to look and see
That nobody stood at the back of me;
But I thought once more: 'Nay, I'll not unvision
20   A shape which, somehow, there may be.'
So I went on softly from the glade,
And left her behind me throwing her shade,
As she were indeed an apparition—
My head unturned lest my dream should fade.

The first two, and the last two lines of Lord Herbert's Elegy are resigned and serene; the last 'alas!' balances the first, with a suggestion of harmony achieved through suffering and faith. A quietly impassioned rhetoric controls the poem's development. Its mood is poignant, but very far removed from despair.

The poem unfolds mainly by way of questions addressed to the dead woman. These are rhetorical questions in that they are not designed, clearly, to receive an answer; yet equally clearly, they *could* not be answered in simple terms, and this, in a sense, is their force. If the asking is simple, with the special simplicity of human hopes and fears, the riddle of 'eternal night' presses beyond the known limits of thought. Are the questions really addressed to the dead woman? The answer to this is by no means easy to define. In part, the poem is a deeply personal meditation, in which the speaker's questions obliquely reflect the strength of his love and grief; in this sense, it is the kind of anguished personal communing with the dead which we need no gloss to understand. But in part, also, the poem is addressed to God, or to the enigmatic universe standing between ourselves and God. 'What is the meaning of life?', it also asks.

Technically, the poem is a series of metaphysical conceits, a series of exaggerations and extravagances which belie, or appear to belie, the coolly logical progress of the thought. This logic has, in fact, the 'pseudo' quality which I. A. Richards noted as a quality of many metaphysical poems. Our response shapes itself not, in the first place, to any rational appraisal of the ideas, but to the intensity of lived experience which these ideas powerfully and obliquely convey. The poem raises the tradition of extravagant praise, for instance, to a pitch which is ostensibly blasphemous (as Courtly Love, with its divinization of the lady, was blasphemous), yet which strikes us rather, in its agonised honesty and humility, as profoundly devout. It is not only the explicit pleas for enlightenment ('Tell us, at least, we pray') which convey this impression, but the whole mood in which the poet writes. The phrase 'low and earthly stage' suggests a perspective which is genuinely, and not just strategically, religious. The 'stage' is a setting for dramatic enactment only one degree removed from ritual; the lady's death becomes a kind of parable or *exemplum*, played out before us all. The word 'ow'd' suggests, moreover, some deep-seated accountability in the material world which justifies such anguished questionings in the soul. Like Bishop Henry King in *The Exequy*, the poet searches a handful of dust for the riches which must one day, or in some manner, be rendered back.

The stated argument itself, however, is not to be taken at face-value, unless we wish something very like nonsense to emerge. In stanza 2, the poet's conceit is that the lady 'chose' her death—chose it not suicidally, of course, but because she was (by implication) too good to live, and because, as deity, the privilege of choosing 'an endless heritage' was hers by right. Nevertheless, her earthly beauties cannot be wasted, and so the further conceit develops, that she replenishes the whole of the 'natural' creation with the colour and vigour of her bodily life. Were this not so, would not the whole creation have gone into mourning? (as it did for instance, for three hours, on the death of Christ). We see from this, indeed, that the dead lady's beauty *must* have passed into the natural world, for how otherwise could its continuing loveliness be explained?

This, very basically, is what the poem *says*; but the poetic

74

force is in the way that the saying takes place. The extravagance is, as we have seen, in the metaphysical tradition, which permits an interplay of strange and finally untenable ideas in the service of deep and often universal emotional truth. The line of questioning will remind us, no doubt, of many other such poems. Carew's '*A Song*', for example, begins:

> Ask me no more where Jove bestowes,
> When June is past, the fading rose:
> For in your beauties orient deep,
> These Flowers as in their causes sleep . . .

In Carew's poem, the notion is apparently the reverse of Lord Herbert's, in that the vitality of dead Nature passes into and enriches the living lady; but the essential nature of the conceit, the acceptance of a world in which the Lady is divine and all beauty resides in her almost as in a Platonic Ideal, is precisely the same. Another comparison, with Marvell's '*The Picture of Little T.C. in a Prospect of Flowers*' (printed on page 104) takes us a little farther along the path. Marvell's little girl, like Eve in her Garden before the Fall, is innocent, and so revivifying to the life of the natural world. The divinity of goodness is embodied in this notion; and we are reminded, especially by Marvell's sombre last stanza, of the persistent pagan and Christian myths of natural renewal through the death of a god. Thus, the notion in Lord Herbert's Elegy of the dead lady as a divinity replenishing the life of nature is not only an extravagant conceit used to convey the poet's personal emotions, but also a serious and persistent theme in the religious thinking of the western world. The hierarchical references throughout the poem reinforce this thought. When the Lady as source of Order dies, chaos must return unless some further factor intervenes—hence the reference to nature's 'proper Laws', and the discovery of a sufficient 'cause' why these should not have been 'broke' (compare with this the use of 'causes' in the last line of the extract from Carew's

'*A Song*' printed above). In addition, the lady's *right* to eternal vitality is witnessed by the active role ascribed to her throughout the poem—choosing to die, delighting 'no more to stay', restoring, vouchsafing, enriching, all gracious as well as life-giving acts. There is in this, indeed, a major paradox, since though the occasion of the poet's grief is the lady's death, our impression of her in the poem remains one of triumphant life. There are no odours of the tomb or charnel-house; no sugges-tion, such as we get in the Hardy poem following, of a wraith-like existence only in the memory of those who survive.

What we find, in short, is a very delicate balance of the personal against the universal; of the poet's personal grief at the lady's physical death against the universal faith in her immor-tality. The complexity comes, as very often in metaphysical poems, from the union of a technique which thrives on extrava-gant ideas with a theology that offers its own apparent extrava-gances in such a crisis—fertility myths, Platonic idealism, the resurrection of the body—as so many bridges across the abyss.

And so one can detect in the poem two main strands. In one obvious and important sense, the stated arguments of the poem need have *no* theological or intellectual validity, or none which a particular reader might acknowledge, for the poem to establish itself as memorable and great. We can say that the arguments are pseudo-arguments adopted as part of the normal meta-physical strategy; that they convey to us the poet's deep and personal feelings, and that in doing this they do all we can, or wish to, ask. We can place the reality of the poem as micro-cosmic instead of macrocosmic, and gloss it thus: it is a painful and universal truth that our personal world can be shattered by the death of a loved person whose life has given it meaning and warmth; but a truth also that the memory of such a person can revivify our personal world, however painfully, through the very qualities which grief attests. A modern reader is apt, perhaps, to concentrate upon this aspect of the poem, and find its validity here, rather than in the theological suggestions and implications behind the conceits. To take this view is, however, to adapt the poem to the twentieth century so fully that we fail to perceive its peculiar balance of strengths. In the seventeenth century it came more naturally than it does today to relate personal loves and griefs to the Order of Creation itself. Clearly, this can be seen to reflect belief in a Universe which cares for the individual human being so fully that immortality is his expectation, and Heaven or Hell the ultimate measure of his deeds. Given this belief, no theological extravagance can be ruled out; to develop the belief through conceits and paradoxes, as Lord Herbert does here, is neither as wilfully unrealistic nor as essentially blasphemous as it may seem. And no less clearly, it can be seen that belief in an Eternal Order holds personal grief in a distinctive balance with faith. It removes the deepest and bitterest sting of bereavement with the offer of reunion beyond the grave. It asserts, in short, that the mystery of death is not beyond explanation—though the pain of not entirely knowing the explanation remains as, of course, does the pain of the actual bereavement itself. This balance is reflected very precisely in the co-existence of quietly controlled questions with extravagantly developed ideas, of very simple language and rhythms with a very complex exploration of grief.

What needs to be said, then, is that though the feeling of the poet for the dead woman in no way depends upon the validity of his religious beliefs, the interdependence of feelings and belief cannot be simply overlooked; otherwise, would the poem not be far nearer, as Hardy's is, to despair? Lord Herbert is asserting that the lady really did incarnate 'Knowledge and Love', and that these qualities, reflected in man, the image of God, are the true springs of life. So the poem merges personal anguish in a kind of trans-personal faith. The 'I' of the first line is also the 'us' of line 10 and of the last stanza; he is Everyman—every Christian man—confronted with love and loss. This, no doubt, is why the modulation of 'us' from object to subject in the penultimate line seems so peculiarly right, despite its defiance of the grammatical norm. In this last modulation, the poet sinks his personal grief into the universal hope of all mankind; the poem moves to its quiet and tranquil end.

The second of these two poems, by Thomas Hardy, has certain obvious affinities with the first. In subject it is also elegiac, the expression of one man's love for a dead woman. And technically, it develops like Lord Herbert's Elegy, through questions addressed to the dead woman—questions which also employ untenable ideas (here, however, fully recognised as untenable) as the reflection of emotional truth. These similarities are clearly important, yet our earliest (and lasting) impression is likely to be of profound dissimilarities between the two. At very first sight, Hardy's poem has an almost Pre-Raphaelite air. The incantatory tone, the use of apparently conventional words like 'broods' and 'lone', the reference to the 'Druid stone' with its gothic and morbid associations, all point to the late nineteenth century as a possible date. Clearly the poet's sensibility is deeply romantic; this poem is far more *purely* personal than Lord Herbert's, in that Hardy relates his suffering not to the Order of Creation as traditionally conceived, but to the emptiness of the universe for one to whom no faith is left. The quality of emotional honesty can be detected in both poems, and so can the quest for a resignation by which it is possible to live. But whereas Lord Herbert's patience, as one senses it in the poem, is Christian, Hardy's, like Matthew Arnold's in *The Scholar Gipsy*, is 'too close neighbour to despair'.

'*The Shadow on the Stone*' belongs in fact not to the late nineteenth century, but to the period shortly after Hardy's wife Emma died in 1912, when he wrote a number of poems in memory of her. Like most of these poems, '*The Shadow on the Stone*' is not as simple as it appears. To a casual reader it may seem crudely written, since, though the words are simple and the images at first sight familiar, there are pitfalls for a conventional or sluggish mind. It could be suggested, for instance, that the phrase 'back of me' (line 18) is clumsy, and that Hardy might have been forced into it by the facile need for a rhyme. If this were true, it would indeed be a serious flaw; but one knows it is not true, as soon as one even starts to respond to the flavour of Hardy's verse. In an earlier poem, 'The Impercipient', Hardy uses a similarly inverted phrase, 'heart of mine'; he is present at a Cathedral service as an unbeliever, and he is wondering why the Christians, if they take their creed at all seriously, do not have more charity towards himself:

> Since heart of mine knows not that ease
>   Which they know; since it be
> That He who breathes All's Well to these
>   Breathes no All's-Well to me,
> My lack might move their sympathies
>   And Christian charity!

That 'heart of mine' establishes itself with a sharp poignancy that no simple analysis can elucidate. There is the realisation that it is the only heart he has, which will one day fail him, but the realisation equally that it is *his* heart, to which he can only be true. The heart as a physical organ which wears out, and the heart as a symbol of total emotional integrity, are wholly united in the syntactical inversion, perhaps by way of the nuances of acceptance and resignation conveyed by the surrounding texture of the verse. Similarly in '*The Shadow on the Stone*' the phrase 'back of me' resonates with Hardy's unique, unmistakeable voice. The very lack of urbanity is, paradoxically it may seem, part of the lyrical music and tenderness, the absolute authenticity of expression and thought. Throughout the poem, the rhythms move subtly and delicately with the meaning; one has to grasp the poem's meaning, and its nuances of meaning, before the reading voice can be certain how this or that phrase should sound. The poem's sweetness and delicacy is fully apparent, indeed, only to a reader who has entered so fully into it that the superficial criticisms of tortuousness or clumsiness will have faded from his mind. In this, it is not unlike the Cavatina of Beethoven's Opus 130, or the marvellous slow movement of Schubert's Opus 163.

The mood of the poem is indeed slow; Hardy is caught unawares by a moment of remembrance, set off by the shadow of a tree swaying in the wind; the poem develops from this, and the *sense* of being caught unawares, of following a train of thought that appears to come effortlessly and inevitably from an initial experience, is the experience which the poem's rhythm and music convey. The poet is fully aware of the physical cause of the shadow, and never for one moment imagines that a 'real' visitation has occurred. Yet such is the bent of the human mind under the sharp remembrance of things past, that he half-believes his wife has come back to him from the shades, familiar and close as in the days of first love. One says 'half-believes', but this phrase little more than approximates to that state of consciousness which most of us can more easily recall than describe. It is a state, certainly, which we associate with that late nineteenth-century no-man's land of religious doubt where so many uneasy Christians and reluctant agnostics met; and associate most of all, perhaps, with Hardy himself, as an outstanding example of the deeply serious Victorian unbeliever, torn with longing for the hopes and pieties which his reason rejects. 'The Impercipient' illustrates such a condition of mind. It is also seen in this beautiful little poem 'The Oxen', where the agony of a whole generation is expressed:

> Christmas Eve, and twelve of the clock.
>   'Now they are all on their knees,'
> An elder said as we sat in a flock
>   By the embers in hearthside ease.

We pictured the meek mild creatures where
    They dwelt in their strawy pen,
Nor did it occur to one of us there
    To doubt they were kneeling then.

So fair a fancy few would weave
    In these years! Yet, I feel,
If someone said on Christmas Eve,
    'Come; see the oxen kneel

'In the lonely barton by yonder coomb
    Our childhood used to know,'
I should go with him in the gloom,
    Hoping it might be so.

In 'The Shadow on the Stone' Hardy's half-belief operates in a more personal way. The poem is set in that hinterland where the mind can still explore, and even encourage, its emotional longings, neither departing from honesty, nor relinquishing one final hope. It offers us 'half-belief' as a tormenting, but not ignoble state; a state, moreover, which none of us can wholly evade under the experience of love and loss, however large or small our own religious hope may be.

The progress of the poem is fascinating to trace. Whereas Lord Herbert's questions in 'Elegy over a Tomb' take the form of poetic conceits, Hardy's questions are those which rise spontaneously to the suffering mind. First, the poet says, he 'stopped and looked' at the shifting shadows; this is a willed act as yet, with little felt significance, a mere pause, during the course of a country walk, before one of nature's normal, but pleasing, effects. But almost at once, the 'rhythmic swing' suggests associations beyond itself. The shadow, says Hardy,

    shaped in my imagining
To the shade that a well-known head and shoulders
    Threw there when she was gardening.

The 'it' turns into 'she'; and the very familiarity of past events that have taken place on this spot makes the transition easy to achieve. The 'rhythmic swing' need not even induce a mild hypnosis for this to happen, since it is a normal illusion played by memory itself. The phrase 'shaped in my imagining' records the poet's awareness of his own contribution; it is a phrase implying no transcendental notion of imagination as a revelation of truth, but only that familiar colouring of association cast over external objects under the stress of emotion which Wordsworth and Coleridge called 'fancy', and which any reader will recognise as a usual operation of the mind. The word 'shade' introduces, however, a beautifully judged ambiguity. The 'shade' is still the 'shadow', the physical image thrown by the tree, but it also becomes 'shade' in the sense of 'ghost', with all the added associations of that idea. We recall the shadowy world of Hades, where Orpheus went to seek Euridyce among the dead—a myth which delicately underlies this poem, counterpointing it with poignant ironies from an earlier world.

So in stanza 2 the poet is ready to say 'I thought'; and 'thought', again, is a word marvellously poised. It can mean 'imagined' in the sense that 'imagining' has already established, the 'imagining' of memory reaching back until past and present begin to blend; but it can, too, mean 'believed'. The poet's longing tugs him as far towards this second meaning as he can honestly go; and it is precisely our sense of the distance of this, how far he *can* go before he encounters the great and unbridgeable gulf, which the poet's lyrical music enacts. The second line of stanza 2 has, for those with biographical knowledge, a hidden depth. For the final years of their married life, Hardy and his wife had been estranged. They had lived together in one house scarcely on speaking terms. It was only Emma's death which broke down for Hardy the recent past and restored, in full tide, the memory of earlier love. Hardy had, indeed, 'learned to lack' his earlier love in her lifetime: years of bitter erosion are contained in the 'long', and not simply the subjectively long period since her death. The shade from the past is therefore twice inaccessible to him, by the history of their life together as it turned out to be, as well as by the intervention of death. There is yet a further irony, in retrospect, when one remembers a main cause of the estrangement. Emma was embittered and scornful about Hardy's agnosticism; about the very quality of painful honesty in him which was to make his poems about her death so decisively great.

It is at this point in the poem that Hardy moves on to 'I said': with most moving delicacy he has now sufficiently suspended disbelief to speak back to his young wife over the gulf of the years, knowing, indeed, that there is no one there to hear or answer, yet still able to say 'I am *sure*'. The word 'sure' is the 'sure' of last-ditch hope, the hope retained, for instance, in the last line of 'The Oxen', 'Hoping it might be true'. What it means, if one can be forgiven the necessary crudity of translation, is something like: 'I wish so much you were here; if wishes were magic you surely would be'. He is even sure enough to ask a question, 'Though how do you get into this old track?' But, as fully expected (our more normal 'sureness'), to this there is no reply; and the poet now has it in his power to disillusion himself finally by looking to *see*, but this final violation of hope he cannot make. The word 'my belief' returns, tinged with the specific irony of the situation itself—an irony marvellously caught up in the word 'nothing', and its implications. If the 'belief' is not true, if she is not there behind him and never can be again, is 'nothing' really the name for all the emotional longing that is thereby denied?

Stanza 3 carries the implications of this still farther:

> Yet I wanted to look and see
> That nobody stood at the back of me;
> But I thought once more: 'Nay, I'll not unvision
> A shape which, somehow, there may be.'

The personal anguish seems perfected in these lines. To 'look and see' is, at one level, the whole tenor of Hardy's honesty, his passionate determination to believe nothing hopeful that cannot be proved: 'proved', that is to say, not by logic or empiricism, but by the knowledge of reality which our experience has taught us to hold. So 'wanted' is, in a deep sense, the correct word; yet is this not the most painful, the most ambiguous of all 'wanting'?—for truth against comfort, for bleak reality against the one final hope?

The poet, after this, 'thought once more'; and his resolve captures, especially in that wonderfully precise 'somehow', the whole search in a world of half-belief for some valid charm against despair. So the poet's act, when he makes it, is that of leaving without looking back; but the curious verbal inversions of the last four lines take us still more subtly into the world of his doubt. The 'softly' suggests that the poet leaves on tip-toe, for all the world as though he were the ghost, and she the creature of flesh and blood who must not be disturbed; and this hint is taken up in the line following, where 'she' becomes for a moment almost solid—the final reality remaining when he has gone. But 'throwing her shade' restores, through the word 'shade', the balance of truth; and the line 'As she were indeed an apparition' offers the final surprising turn. In emphasis, it suggests an entire reversal of the meaning it must contain: as if she is a reality whom Hardy's doubts have reduced to an apparition, rather than a 'nobody' whom his half-belief has conjured up.

The last line, in its haunting simplicity, needs little comment; the dignity of the one last evasion speaks for itself. Yet a casual reader might miss the suggestion of Orpheus seeking Euridyce among the dead, which runs just under the poem, and comes near to the surface at the end. In the old myth, Euridyce really was following Orpheus, but Orpheus lost her by the forbidden act of looking back. In Hardy's poem, Emma is not there, and Hardy's success in not looking back does not work the magic in reverse. Returning to fetch the dead, in whatever manner, one can never be 'sure'.

Can a final balance between the two poems we have been considering be made? It does not seem possible. Both are great poems, but great in almost wholly different ways, despite the superficial similarities of subject and technique. Most readers are likely to prefer one to the other in the last resort, but this preference will be more a matter of the individual temperament than of 'literary merit'. Undoubtedly one could find two other poems of faith and doubt where one could say, *this* is the good poem, *that* the bad; and where this judgment would have nothing to do with what the critic personally 'believed'. But here, we have the more rewarding instance of two poems which achieve greatness on their own terms.

Both poems (one might say in summary) reflect states of feeling through the interplay of finally untenable ideas. In Lord Herbert's poem, this is achieved inside the 'metaphysical' tradition, which allows true emotions to be conveyed obliquely by way of strange and exaggerated ideas—though the ideas themselves have a certain validity also, as we have pointed out, through the theological complex to which they refer. In Hardy's poem, the ideas are those prompted by desire for reunion with the beloved after death, and here the degree to which they are untenable is well known to the poet himself: it is, as we have seen, the emotional force of the poem itself.

Questions

1. The authors refer in passing to 'Courtly Love'. What were the main characteristics of Courtly Love in mediaeval and Tudor verse? (The best introduction to this important subject is still C. S. Lewis' *The Allegory of Love*.)

2. 'The hierarchical references throughout the poem reinforce the thought'. What do you understand by 'hierarchical'? Give a brief account of the ideas of 'hierarchy' prevalent in feudal and

Tudor England. (A useful book to consult is *The Elizabethan World Picture*, by E. M. W. Tillyard.)

3. What do you understand by the terms 'microcosmic' and 'macrocosmic'? What do the authors mean by the term 'a pseudo-argument'?

4. 'Most readers are likely to prefer one poem to the other in the last resort, but this preference will be more a matter of the individual temperament than of "literary merit".' Do you prefer one poem to the other? If so, do you agree that this is for personal rather than for aesthetic reasons?

5. Consider the use of rhetorical questions in both poems. Do you agree with what has been said about them?

6. Consider the precise implications in 'Elegy over a Tomb' of:

    (*a*) 'prove' (line 5)
    (*b*) 'ow'd' (line 11)
    (*c*) 'some cause' (line 25)
    (*d*) 'intend' (line 34)

7. Consider the precise implications in *'The Shadow on the Stone'* of:

    (*a*) 'imagining' (line 6)
    (*b*) 'old track' (line 12)
    (*c*) 'discover' (line 15)
    (*d*) 'unvision' (line 19)
    (*e*) 'dream' (line 24)

8. Write a critique of (or discuss in class) Hardy's poem 'The Oxen', which is printed in full in this analysis.

Exercise
7

A comparison of Thom Gunn's '*On the Move*' with Ted Hughes'
'*Six Young Men*', with questions.

Thom Gunn's '*On the Move*'
'Man, you gotta Go'

The blue jay scuffling in the bushes follows
Some hidden purpose, and the gust of birds
That spurts across the field, the wheeling swallows,
Have nested in the trees and undergrowth.
Seeking their instinct, or their poise, or both,
One moves with an uncertain violence
Under the dust thrown by a baffled sense
Or the dull thunder of approximate words.

On motor cycles, up the road, they come:
Small, black, as flies hanging in heat, the Boys,
Until the distance throws them forth, their hum
Bulges to thunder held by calf and thigh.
In goggles, donned impersonality,
In gleaming jackets trophied with the dust,
They strap in doubt—by hiding it, robust—
And almost hear a meaning in their noise.

Exact conclusion of their hardiness
Has no shape yet, but from known whereabouts
They ride, direction where the tires press.
They scare a flight of birds across the field:
Much that is natural, to the will must yield.

Men manufacture both machine and soul,
And use what they imperfectly control
To dare a future from the taken routes.

It is a part solution, after all.
One is not necessarily discord
On earth; or damned because, half animal,
One lacks direct instinct, because one wakes
Afloat on movement that divides and breaks.
One joins the movement in a valueless world,
Choosing it, till, both hurler and the hurled,
One moves as well, always toward, toward.

A minute holds them, who have come to go:
The self-defined, astride the created will
They burst away; the towns they travel through
Are home for neither bird nor holiness,
For birds and saints complete their purposes.
At worst, one is in motion; and at best,
Reaching no absolute, in which to rest,
One is always nearer by not keeping still.

Ted Hughes' 'Six Young Men'

The celluloid of a photograph holds them well,—
Six young men, familiar to their friends.
Four decades that have faded and ochre-tinged
This photograph have not wrinkled the faces or the hands.
Though their cocked hats are not now fashionable,
Their shoes shine. One imparts an intimate smile,
One chews a grass, one lowers his eyes, bashful,
One is ridiculous with cocky pride—
Six months after this picture they were all dead.

All are trimmed for a Sunday jaunt. I know
That bilberried bank, that thick tree, that black wall,

Which are there yet and not changed. From where these sit
You hear the water of seven streams fall
To the roarer in the bottom, and through all
The leafy valley a rumouring of air go.
Pictured here, their expressions listen yet,
And still that valley has not changed its sound
Though their faces are four decades under the ground.

This one was shot in an attack and lay
Calling in the wire, then this one, his best friend,
Went out to bring him in and was shot too;
And this one, the very moment he was warned
From potting at tin-cans in no-man's land,
Fell back dead with his rifle-sights shot away.
The rest, nobody knows what they came to,
But come to the worst they must have done, and held it
Closer than their hope; all were killed.

Here see a man's photograph,
The locket of a smile, turned overnight
Into the hospital of his mangled last
Agony and hours; see bundled in it
His mightier-than-a-man dead bulk and weight:
And on this one place which keeps him alive
(In his Sunday best) see fall war's worst
Thinkable flash and rending, onto his smile
Forty years rotting into soil.

That man's not more alive whom you confront
And shake by the hand, see hale, hear speak loud,
Than any of these six celluloid smiles are,
Nor prehistoric or fabulous beast more dead;
No thought so vivid as their smoking blood:
To regard this photograph might well dement,
Such contradictory permanent horrors here

Smile from the single exposure and shoulder out
One's own body from its instant and heat.

Thom Gunn's poem is about young men on motor-bikes, the
first young men in a line which has mutated through ton-up
boys to rockers, and beyond, since the poem was written. In
the earlier 1950's, the cult was exemplified in *The Wild Ones*, a
Marlon Brando film which was shown in Cambridge by special
licence at about the time when Thom Gunn was a student there,
but was banned nationally because of its possibly unsettling effect
upon the young. Still earlier memories might be stirred by this
poem—the escort of motor-cyclists depicted with such sinister
power in Cocteau's *Orfée*; and Hitler's youth, of course, muscular
and well drilled in their black uniforms and jack-boots.

The first stanza is technically very interesting, in that the boys,
and Thom Gunn's attitude to them, are foreshadowed before
they appear. The first two lines announce one of Gunn's characteristic preoccupations, the sense of a 'hidden purpose' behind
apparently random movements. The blue jay is 'scuffling', yet
the vagueness recorded by this word is false. The next image is
of 'the gust of birds', the 'wheeling swallows', a kind of brief
revelation of purpose and energy combined ('gust' is especially
vivid and accurate). In the second part of this stanza, the poet
envies the birds 'their instinct, or their poise, or both'. The 'One'
in line 6 (he reappears later in stanza 4) may be man in general,
seeking some gift in which the birds are his natural superior, or
he may be, more particularly, the poet, engaged in 'the intoler-
able wrestle with words and meanings' (Gunn probably recalled
T. S. Eliot's phrase in *Four Quartets*). The literal sense allows both
possibilities, since words are one of the chief marks of man's
supposed superiority to the beasts. Already the imagery ('uncertain violence', 'dust thrown', 'dull thunder') prefigures the
roar of the boys coming along the road, the central human
image of the poem, and suggests a parallel between the movement of the boys and the poet's search for meaning.

The motor-cyclists appear, therefore, on a scene which has been carefully prepared (in miniature, the implications of the first stanza might remind us of the opening of Hopkins' *The Wreck of the Deutschland*, where the rhythms of storm and shipwreck establish themselves around important ideas before the actual storm and shipwreck occur). From the start, we are simultaneously aware of two levels in the poem, the literal meaning, where the ethos of the boys is very vividly and physically evoked, and the intellectual meaning, where the boys become symbols of something very close to a philosophy of life. How closely, and in what ways, does the poet identify himself with the boys? How are we drawn in as readers?

The image with which the boys are actually introduced, in the second line of the second stanza, is acutely distasteful; 'small' and 'black' are unattractive words, while the 'flies hanging in heat' may afflict us with a sense of nausea. This impression of something insect and alien is partly physical; the goggles and black leather, seen from a distance, disguise individual, and even human, identity. But as the boys come nearer, this first impression yields to a sense of their power. The line 'Bulges to thunder held by calf and thigh' is both muscular and erotic. The physical mastery of their motor-bikes brings the boys a power comparable to that of the 'gust of birds' of the first stanza (though with one major difference, which the next stanza takes as its theme). The first image of 'flies hanging in heat' is followed by 'gleaming jackets trophied with the dust'. By risking their lives, the boys take on heroic stature, which we ordinary men fear and admire, mistrust and envy—associating them both with the hated Nazis and with our own war heroes, as well (no doubt) as with our personal inadequacies in the face of violence, and our dreams of escape. The phrase 'donned impersonality' very precisely defines the kind of romanticism associated with the boys, the glamour of individuality sunk in a uniform, and so transcended; a collective ideal and way of life.

The last two lines of the second stanza identify the boys more closely with modern intellectuals, in their parallel search for identity and meaning; the debilitating effect of 'doubt' is a commonplace of modern thought. The boys control their doubt as they control their machines, by muscle and will, 'And almost hear a meaning in their noise'. The compressed suggestiveness of this line becomes fully apparent only if one attempts a paraphrase. Clearly the poet has existentialist theories in mind, perhaps Camus' belief in commitment to energy as a good-in-itself, a means of conferring *enough* meaning on existence for life to continue, whatever the remaining areas of doubt.

The third stanza develops such philosophical ideas more directly. The boys, like the blue jay, follow 'some hidden purpose,' which may never be known, yet which keeps them 'on the move'. It is undoubtedly ironic that the human will is associated with something 'manufactured', both in the machines that the boys ride and, more importantly, in their 'soul'. The birds are scared by the noise of the motor-bikes, and the wry comment 'Much that is natural, to the will must yield' suggests that though the boys move with energy, they do this not by natural 'instinct' or 'poise' like the birds, but by naked will: a will linked to mechanisation, and potentially hostile to the poise of 'nature' itself. Even so, the word 'dare' is more appropriate to the boys than to the birds, and the *glamour* of movement belongs specifically to them. And, says the poet, 'It is a part solution, after all'—a part solution to our more human predicament of 'discord' and damnation (strong words), our lack of a 'sense of movement' like the birds. So the fourth stanza reintroduces the 'One' of the first stanza, whom we now see to be the poet himself, and those who are in philosophic agreement with him; and the poem arrives at its central idea. In a 'valueless world' it is still possible to make valuable choices, to move fast and meaningfully without a map.

The last stanza opens with something like a snapshot: 'A

minute holds them, who have come to go'. And then the boys
roar away, through towns which, says the poet, 'Are home for
neither bird nor holiness'. The introduction of 'holiness' here,
and of 'saints' in the next line, has been felt by some readers to
be inappropriate. The idea, presumably, is that 'saints' do achieve
'natural' instinct or poise (or both) like the birds, but that they
are too few and far between to count. This may or may not be
true, but the poem has nowhere prepared us for it, and it might
not be thought, therefore, to carry much weight. On the other
hand, it could be argued that the casual introduction of saints
into this stanza, without preparation, suggests how irrelevant
religious attitudes have become in the modern world. The cer-
tainty of the saint is as impossible to achieve today as the natural
instincts of the birds. The main conclusion, of course, is in favour
of the boys, whose implied judgment against twentieth-century
cities is seen to be truer than the answering judgments of conventional city dwellers against the boys. The towns they roar
through are the waste-lands of subtopia, places like the New
Town in Eliot George's *The Leather Boys* where apathy and
dullness force energy, if it is to manifest itself at all, into revolt.
One of the unstated factors in this poem is Gunn's rejection of
subtopia; it is for this reason that the boys become symbols of
his own revolt.

But the meaning of the poem cannot be reduced to purely
intellectual terms; the physical power and glamour of boys and
machines is the main impression conveyed. Nor can one simplify
even the intellectual meaning into Stevenson's 'To travel hope-
fully is a better thing than to arrive'. The motto 'Man, you
gotta Go' suggests some restless compulsion to movement, a
drive that links Gunn with the Beat poets, despite the entire
dissimilarity in technique. One feels that he is *driven*, that he has
this in common with the boys.

This brings us, finally, to the poem's form. Like most of
Gunn's poems, 'On the Move' is metrically strict, with the

rhyme scheme 'abaccddb'. Most of the rhymes are full or near-full, and where they are not, the half-rhyme is part of a recurring onomatopoeia (we hear and *see* the motor-bikes in the sounds and movements of the verse). The fact that line 4 in each stanza does not rhyme 'b' but introduces the new 'c' rhyme is important; it ensures that though all of the stanzas except the fourth demand a substantial pause after the fourth line, we realise that the meaning is still incomplete. It is of interest, too, that the final line should produce the very delayed rhyme to the second line, where it comes both as a distant echo and a full-stop. This delayed rhyme gives a sense of completeness to the statement of the stanza.

The use of language is very precise. There is no padding of any kind but, on the contrary, a remarkable compression, which close reading serves to underline. The almost classical control of syntax and imagery makes it easy to see why Gunn is so often considered to be a 'Movement' poet, but the violence of the material which he expresses through this form, the underlying existentialism of thought and, importantly, the energy generated by the poem, are very distinctively his own.

The points of comparison in theme between Gunn's 'On the Move' and Ted Hughes' 'Six Young Men' are at once obvious. Ted Hughes' poem, like Thom Gunn's, deals with a group of young men involved in violence, though with a difference: these young men do not choose violence but are chosen by it, and all are dead forty years before the poem begins. Our main concern, as before, is to sense how the poet relates himself to these young men and what significance he finds in them.

The first stanza, unlike Gunn's, moves straight into the main theme; the poet is looking at and musing upon a photograph. Almost at once we are aware of a great *pressure* behind the vocabulary; every word is precise and relevant, as in the former poem, but one also feels an added richness of allusion. The word 'holds', for instance, implies more than the obvious meaning,

94

and its full sense is only made clear when the poem is finished; we shall return to this in a moment, but it is not an overstatement to say that the word 'holds', in this context, contains the emotional force of the poem. The phrase 'familiar to their friends' establishes, with admirable economy, the essential *ordinariness* of the young men, an impression which the short but vivid descriptions in lines 5-8 reinforce. Whereas Thom Gunn's young men are rebels against social deadness, Ted Hughes' belong to a rich, if unspectacular, common life. The 'intimate smile', lowered eyes, 'cocky pride' relate them very precisely to family and friends; and the word 'ridiculous' is especially telling: its overtone of affectionate acceptance establishes very exactly the working-class community from which they come. Only the last line makes specific that they are dead, but we have already suspected this from the powerfully compressed third and fourth lines. Ted Hughes captures here, with rare economy, the feelings we have all had before those photographs of the dead in the First World War—the faces and hands unwrinkled, the smile unchanged, yet the image already fading, in human memory, like the celluloid itself. It is instructive to compare these two lines with the well-known stanza from Laurence Binyon's 'For the Fallen', a poem written soon after the First World War ended, and still recited piously when the Day of Remembrance comes round:

> They shall grow not old as we that are left grow old:
> Age shall not weary them, nor the years condemn.
> At the going down of the sun and in the morning
> We will remember them.

Could Binyon have been aware of the echo from *Antony and Cleopatra* when he wrote this?—Most of us today dislike Binyon's specious rhetoric and emotional dishonesty—its glamorised slaughter, its offer of an unexamined immortality, its exaggeration of our human power to remember and care. In contrast,

Ted Hughes explores the reality of the unwrinkled faces and hands, the human remembering, with terrifying exactness; the full implications of 'holds' in the first line already start to become clear. The photograph 'holds' them in the obvious sense of a good likeness, but it 'holds' them, more basically, against oblivion. It is, says the poet later, 'this one place which keeps him alive'—but the qualification of the life that they still have there, the very minimal and ironic nature of such holding as there can be, is the tragic understanding from which the poem evolves. The 'faded and ochre-tinged' celluloid fittingly reflects the minds of those who live on; the image alters, grief fades with fashion (the word 'fashionable' in line 5 carries a precise irony); the hold on immortality is as precarious as memory and time.

The second stanza moves into a pastoral mood, as the poet recalls the setting where the photograph was taken, and his own childhood associations with the spot. This is not unlike the opening of Wordsworth's *Tintern Abbey*, where a place with powerful childhood associations is revisited in later life. One realises, as one part of the theme of transience, that Ted Hughes is too young to have known the dead men himself; he does, however, know the place where they were photographed, though his own powerful childhood memories belong to a time after the young men were killed. The main theme of the unchanged (or comparatively unchanged) place held in balance against totally changed personal histories develops more quietly here—the place still there, serene and apparently the same; the young men gone; the poet himself changed since the beauty of the place first entered into his mind. Only the last line returns us, savagely, to the fact of death (as all the last lines do, including, in an altered form, the last line of the final stanza itself).

In the third stanza the poet's meditation moves to another moment, the moment of death for the young men, as far as he can reconstruct it from the little that is known. The words 'his best friend' are particularly poignant, with their reference back to 'familiar to their friends' in the first stanza. 'Best' is fully justified by the supreme sacrifice, yet the poet's austerity allows no opportunities for the sentimentality by which we may want to escape. The last three lines have a distancing effect which is strangely moving. And 'held' (like 'holds' in stanza 1) is oddly effective—as though death were more real to them at the end than hope, and in some strange sense the choosing were really their own.

So in the fourth stanza the poet is ready to return to the present, after these two significant excursions into the past; and now he can define further ambiguities in the manner in which the photograph 'holds' the dead men 'well'. In line 5, he pays homage to the larger-than-life quality of the dead, especially of the dead who are victims or heroes of war, and this is a theme which recurs in many of his poems, though always balanced with the awareness of suffering and loss. Yet the photograph does not simply invest the dead with larger-than-life qualities; it invests them also with the ironies by which such permanence is defined. The photograph itself is a victim of war, ravished not only by the natural fading of celluloid, but by 'war's worst Thinkable flash and rending'. 'Thinkable' is the key word here, the reminder that our perceptions themselves are conditioned by associations and thoughts. Thus the 'locket', with its suggestions of a tender keepsake, becomes a 'hospital'; the smile of the dead, though physically unchanged, is changed for those who live on. The knowledge of 'forty years rotting into soil' is inextricably part of their reaction to these faces. Indeed, the word 'rotting', which makes the full horror explicit, emerges from the poet's study of the smile. So even the trivial things in the photograph become a torment, the 'Sunday best' a reminder that they were alive, about their normal business, *then*. The parenthesis 'In his Sunday best' is a kind of microcosm of the poem's tone; seemingly dispassionate, even casual, it is very exact and painful in its effect.

The last stanza comes as a final statement of the 'contradictory permanent horrors' of such a photograph. In the first five lines we are presented with apparent opposites, and the phrase 'single exposure' unites the moment when the photograph was taken (the photographic exposure) with the moment of death, without our even being conscious of a pun. The poem ends, by a further twist, with the deadening power of the dead over the living. The immortality of the dead, as the photograph holds it, is qualified in this final way.

Technically, the poem is a triumph. Ted Hughes, like Thom Gunn, uses a metrical form, but he uses it almost with the freedom of free-verse. In Gunn's poem, the metre directs and controls the tone; in Ted Hughes', the tone tugs constantly against the metre, with an effect of rugged and impressive immediacy (this is the kind of poetry which one seems to overhear).

Which of these two poems do we prefer? Both are very good, as we have tried to show. Both are verbally precise and metrically skilled; both develop complex emotional responses to a situation involving violence; both seem at the end satisfyingly complete. Perhaps the Gunn poem is more open to criticism on its chosen terms: to make the leather-jacketed boys symbolic the poet is forced to oversimplify in several fairly obvious ways. The ordinary social world is toned down to a 'home for neither bird nor holiness'—which justifies the extreme revolt of the boys, but overlooks the very real values expressed by many conventional communities (the values which Ted Hughes, for instance, very economically but surely sketches in as the background of his young men). It is of a piece with Thom Gunn's over-simplification here that the 'saint' should be brought in without due preparation. One senses that the poet's manipulation of his symbols towards an existential 'moral' is somewhat less subtle than his evocation of the physical presence and reality of the boys themselves. With this in mind, it is possible to feel that the poet's identification of himself with the sheer physical glamour of the boys (an identification distanced and modified, of course, by the aesthetic form) does not *exactly* reflect the intellectual framework of the poem. We see the boys from a distance at first, and we remain looking on from the outside. The poet identifies himself with them at the point where his own imagination is fired, but would the boys in any way recognise this picture of themselves? Even if we allow for the fact (as we must) that a poet lends his own gift of articulation to the normally inarticulate, we may wonder whether the boys' way of life is to them, consciously or unconsciously, a search for 'meaning' in quite this way. The answer *may* be that it is—or that it is to some of them (this second possibility must almost certainly be true); yet one feels a difference between the fascination with speed for the boys, and the intellectual quest of the poet.

In Ted Hughes' poem, no such problems arise. There is no overtly philosophical purpose, and the emotional intensity arises wholly from properties in the photograph itself. Once again, we can say that the poet lends his superior gifts of articulation to the rest of us, who must often have felt such emotions. But this time, it is certain that these precisely *are* our emotions; Ted Hughes speaks as directly and powerfully for ordinary humanity contemplating war as Wilfred Owen does in 'Futility' or Yeats in 'Easter 1916' (though naturally the emotional emphases fall differently in all these poets, and perhaps 'ordinary humanity' is too ambiguous a term to use). The implications in 'Six Young Men', at any rate, are moving and unanswerable; whereas Thom Gunn's symbols, though profoundly interesting and lively, may well be questioned when the force of his personal emotional commitment ceases to be felt.

Both of these poems, we would stress, seem to us very powerful.

Questions

1. What is Gunn's 'philosophy' as exemplified in 'On The Move'?

99

2. Do you think the motor-cyclists act as a satisfactory symbol for Gunn's ideas? Does it seem odd to you that he should invest these boys with heroic qualities?

3. Do you know what is meant by 'existentialist theories'?

4. What is your view of Gunn's use of 'holiness' and 'saints' in the last stanza? Are such references appropriate in this context?

5. Describe the use of language whereby Gunn invests the boys with 'physical power and glamour'. What effects are achieved by placing these images of violence in a carefully disciplined stanzaic form?

6. Do the comments on Hughes' poem add anything to your appreciation, or do you feel that any intelligent reader would perceive these meanings?

7. What do you think Hughes means by 'contradictory permanent horrors' (final stanza)? How are the horrors contradictory?

8. Which poem do you prefer? Or do you think this question irrelevant? Do you agree with the adverse comments made on Gunn's poem? Is it possible to argue that Gunn has a precise, lucid concept of heroic action, while Hughes is emotional and confused? Do you agree with the last sentence of the commentary?

9. Do you think comparison between these poems is rewarding, or are the similarities too superficial?

Exercise

8

Shakespeare's Sonnet 73

That time of year thou mayst in me behold,
When yellow leaves, or none, or few, do hang

Upon those boughs which shake against the cold,
Bare ruin'd choirs, where late the sweet birds sang.
In me thou see'st the twilight of such day
As after Sunset fadeth in the West,
Which by and by black night doth take away,
Death's second self, that seals up all in rest.
In me thou see'st the glowing of such fire,
That on the ashes of his youth doth lie,
As the deathbed whereon it must expire,
Consumed with that which it was nourish'd by.
This thou perceiv'st, which makes thy love more strong,
To love that well which thou must leave ere long.

Questions

1. This sonnet is full of apparently conventional images, the yellow leaves of autumn, the sunset fading in the west, the ashes of youth. How does Shakespeare create great poetry out of these?

2. Consider the precise effects of:
   (a) When yellow leaves, or none, or few . . . (line 2)
   (b) Bare ruin'd choirs, where late the sweet birds sang (line 4)
   (c) by and by . . . (line 7)
   (d) Death's second self, that seals up all in rest (line 8).

3. How is the content of this poem affected by the sonnet form? What is the value of the concluding couplet, and the simple words in the last line? Consider the kinds of language and image used throughout. What is their total effect?

4. Elizabethan poets were always writing conventional sonnets about time. Do you think Shakespeare manages to express any personal feeling?

5. How does Shakespeare use Nature to reflect his own state of mind?

6. Choose one other Shakespeare sonnet that seems to you

great, and one Elizabethan sonnet that you think is conventional. Compare and contrast them.

7. How far do you feel that knowledge of other Elizabethan sonnets and of the Elizabethan period in general helps you to appreciate this sonnet?

Exercise
9

(a) From Shakespeare's *Richard II*, Act III, Scene II.

Richard:

No matter where; of comfort no man speak:
Let's talk of graves, of worms, and epitaphs,
Make dust our paper, and with rainy eyes
Write sorrow on the bosom of the earth.
Let's choose executors, and talk of wills:
And yet not so; for what can we bequeath,
Save our deposed bodies to the ground?
Our lands, our lives, and all are Bolingbroke's,
And nothing can we call our own, but Death,
And that small model of the barren Earth,
Which serves as paste, and cover to our bones:
For God's sake let us sit upon the ground,
And tell sad stories of the death of Kings:
How some have been depos'd, some slain in war,
Some haunted by the ghosts they have depos'd,
Some poison'd by their wives, some sleeping kill'd,
All murther'd. For within the hollow Crown
That rounds the mortal temples of a King,
Keeps Death his Court, and there the Antic sits

Scoffing his state, and grinning at his pomp,
Allowing him a breath, a little scene,
To monarchise, be fear'd, and kill with looks,
Infusing him with self and vain conceit,
As if this flesh, which walls about our life,
Were brass impregnable: and humour'd thus,
Comes at the last, and with a little pin
Bores through his castle wall, and farewell King.
Cover your heads, and mock not flesh and blood
With solemn reverence: throw away respect,
Tradition, form, and ceremonious duty,
For you have but mistook me all this while:
I live with bread like you, feel want,
Taste grief, need friends: subjected thus,
How can you say to me, I am a King?

(b) From Marlowe's *Tamburlaine*, *Part I*, Act II, Scene VII:

Tamburlaine:

The thirst of reign and sweetness of a crown,
That caus'd the eldest son of heavenly Ops
To thrust his doting father from his chair,
And place himself in the empyreal Heaven,
Mov'd me to manage arms against thy state.
What better precedent than mighty Jove?
Nature that fram'd us of four elements,
Warring within our breasts for regiment,
Doth teach us all to have aspiring minds:
Our souls, whose faculties can comprehend
The wondrous architecture of the world,
And measure every wand'ring planet's course,
Still climbing after knowledge infinite,
And always moving as the restless spheres,
Wills us to wear ourselves, and never rest,

Until we reach the ripest fruit of all,
That perfect bliss and sole felicity,
The sweet fruition of an earthly crown.

Compare and contrast these two speeches.

Exercise
10

Marvell's '*The Picture of Little T.C. in a Prospect of Flowers*'.

    1   See with what simplicity
        This Nimph begins her golden daies!
        In the green Grass she loves to lie,
        And there with her fair Aspect tames
    5   The Wilder Flow'rs, and gives them names:
        But only with the Roses playes;
                And them does tell
        What Colour best becomes them, and what Smell.

        Who can foretell for what high cause
   10   This Darling of the Gods was born!
        Yet this is She whose chaster Laws
        The wanton Love shall one day fear,
        And, under her command severe,
        See his Bow broke and Ensigns torn.
   15   Happy, who can
        Appease this virtuous Enemy of Man!

        O then let me in time compound,
        And parly with those conquering Eyes;
        Ere they have try'd their force to wound,
   20   Ere, with their glancing wheels, they drive
        In Triumph over Hearts that strive,

And them that yield but more despise.
　　　　Let me be laid,
Where I may see thy Glories from some Shade.

25　Mean time, whilst every verdant thing
　　It self does at thy Beauty charm,
　　Reform the errours of the Spring;
　　Make that the Tulips may have share
　　Of sweetness, seeing they are fair;
30　And Roses of their thorns disarm:
　　　　But most procure
　　That Violets may a longer Age endure.

　　But O young beauty of the Woods,
　　Whom Nature courts with fruits and flow'rs,
35　Gather the Flow'rs, but spare the Buds;
　　Lest *Flora* angry at thy crime,
　　To kill her Infants in their prime,
　　Do quickly make th'Example Yours;
　　　　And, ere we see,
40　Nip in the blossome all our hopes and Thee.

Questions

1. What is the emblematic significance of: the rose, the tulip, the violet?

2. Behind the picture of the little girl in the garden is another picture of Eve in Paradise. Trace the suggestions of this religious idea throughout the poem, and say how it colours the poet's attitude to 'innocence'.

3. Consider the attitude to sexual love that is expressed in this poem.

4. Do you find anything ambiguous or paradoxical in:
　(a) 'Who can foretell for what high cause
　　　　This Darling of the Gods was born!'
　　　and

(b)   'But most procure
That Violets may a longer Age endure'.

5. How would you define Marvell's attitude to Little T.C.?—
and to the particular moment he is observing?

6. What is the effect of the poet's direct address to the child
in the first line of the last stanza?

7. In what way (or ways) is the little girl represented as being
menaced? Consider the poet's warning to her: what is its nature,
and does he really think she could heed it? How far is the passing
of time represented as an inescapable evil?

8. Do you see the poem chiefly as a celebration of Little T.C.,
or as an exploration of the poet's personal reflections on human
life?

9. Consider the precise implications of:

(a) 'simplicity' (line 1)
(b) 'Nimph' and 'golden daies' (line 2)
(c) 'tames' (line 4)
(d) 'gives them names' (line 5)
(e) 'tell' (line 7)
(f) 'The wanton Love' (line 12)
(g) 'virtuous Enemy' (line 16)
(h) 'in time' (line 17)
(i) 'conquering Eyes' (line 18)
(j) 'despise' (line 22)
(k) 'Reform the errours of the Spring' (line 27)
(l) 'thorns' and 'disarm' (line 30)
(m) 'longer Age' (line 32)
(n) 'Nature courts' (line 34)
(o) 'spare the Buds' (line 35)
(p) 'Th'Example' (line 38)
(q) 'Nip in the blossome' (line 40).

Exercise
11

George Herbert's 'Vertue'

Sweet day, so cool, so calm, so bright,
The bridall of the earth and skie:
The dew shall weep thy fall to night;
       For thou must die.

Sweet rose, whose hue angrie and brave
Bids the rash gazer wipe his eye:
Thy root is ever in its grave,
       And thou must die.

Sweet spring, full of sweet dayes and roses,
A box where sweets compacted lie;
My musick shows ye have your closes,
       And all must die.

Onely a sweet and vertuous soul,
Like season'd timber, never gives;
But though the whole world turn to coal,
       Then chiefly lives.

Write an analysis of this poem.

Exercise
12

Milton's 'Paradise Lost', Book IX

404 O much deceav'd, much failing, hapless *Eve*,
     Of thy presum'd return! event perverse!

Thou never from that houre in Paradise
Foundst either sweet repast, or sound repose;
Such ambush hid among sweet Flours and Shades
Waited with hellish rancor imminent
410 To intercept thy way, or send thee back
Despoild of Innocence, of Faith, of Bliss.
For now, and since first break of dawne the Fiend,
Meer Serpent in appearance, forth was come,
And on his Quest, where likeliest he might finde
415 The onely two of Mankinde, but in them
The whole included Race, his purposd prey.
In Bowre and Field he sought, where any tuft
Of Grove or Garden-Plot more pleasant lay,
Thir tendance or Plantation for delight,
420 By Fountain or by shadie Rivulet
He sought them both, but wishd his hap might find
Eve separate, he wishd, but not with hope
Of what so seldom chanc'd, when to his wish,
Beyond his hope, *Eve* separate he spies,
425 Veild in a Cloud of Fragrance, where she stood,
Half spi'd, so thick the Roses bushing round
About her glowd, oft stooping to support
Each Flour of slender stalk, whose head though gay
Carnation, Purple, Azure, or spect with Gold,
430 Hung drooping unsustaind, them she upstaies
Gently with Mirtle band, mindless the while,
Her self, though fairest unsupported Flour,
From her best prop so farr, and storm so nigh.
Neerer he drew, and many a walk travers'd
435 Of stateliest Covert, Cedar, Pine, or Palme,
Then voluble and bold, now hid, now seen
Among thick-woven Arborets and Flours
Imborderd on each Bank, the hand of *Eve*:
Spot more delicious then those Gardens feignd

440 Or of reviv'd *Adonis*, or renownd
  Alcinous, host of old *Laertes* Son,
  Or that, not Mystic, where the Sapient King
  Held dalliance with his faire *Egyptian* Spouse.
  Much he the Place admir'd, the Person more.

445 As one who long in populous City pent,
  Where Houses thick and Sewers annoy the Aire,
  Forth issuing on a Summers Morn to breathe
  Among the pleasant Villages and Farmes
  Adjoind, from each thing met conceaves delight,

450 The smell of Grain, or tedded Grass, or Kine,
  Or Dairie, each rural sight, each rural sound;
  If chance with Nymphlike step fair Virgin pass,
  What pleasing seemd, for her now pleases more,
  Shee most, and in her look summs all Delight.

455 Such Pleasure took the Serpent to behold
  This Flourie Plat, the sweet recess of *Eve*
  Thus earlie, thus alone; her Heav'nly forme
  Angelic, but more soft, and Feminine,
  Her graceful Innocence, her every Aire

460 Of gesture or lest action overawd
  His Malice, and with rapin sweet bereav'd
  His fierceness of the fierce intent it brought:
  That space the Evil one abstracted stood
  From his own evil, and for the time remaind

465 Stupidly good, of enmitie disarmd,
  Of guile, of hate, of envie, of revenge;
  But the hot Hell that alwayes in him burnes,
  Though in mid Heav'n, soon ended his delight,
  And tortures him now more, the more he sees

470 Of pleasure not for him ordaind: then soon
  Fierce hate he recollects, and all his thoughts
  Of mischief, gratulating, thus excites.

Questions

1. Consider the syntax and diction of this passage. Does it seem to you to depart from normal English usage? Say what you understand by the 'heroic' (or 'epic') tradition, and how far you think this is demonstrated here.

Do you think that Milton is at all *personally* present in these lines? Or do you think he is writing solely as the voice of a tradition?

2. How do you feel this relates to the narrative in *Genesis* on which it is based? Explain the references in lines 440–3 to: '*Adonis*', '*Alcinous*', 'old *Laertes* Son', 'Sapient King' and '*Egyptian* Spouse'. What do you think these references add to the passage?

3. Consider lines 404–11. How would you describe the feeling conveyed by these lines? In what sense are they ironic? Consider the use of imagery in these lines, and the use of contrast.

Consider the precise implications of:

    (*a*) 'much deceav'd, much failing' (line 404)
    (*b*) 'presum'd' (line 405)
    (*c*) 'event perverse' (line 405)
    (*d*) 'Such ambush' (line 408)
    (*e*) 'hellish rancor imminent' (line 409)

4. Consider lines 412–443: the irony, the imagery, the use of contrast. How does Milton establish Eve's innocence and beauty? How far does he create the sense that she is a victim? Do you think that what we are made to feel for Eve works for or against the main theological intention of the passage?

Consider the precise implications of:

    (*a*) 'Meer Serpent in appearance' (line 413)
    (*b*) 'The whole included Race, his purposd prey' (line 416)
    (*c*) 'to his wish,/Beyond his hope' (lines 423–4)
    (*d*) 'Half spi'd' (line 426)
    (*e*) 'bushing round/About her glowd' (lines 426–7)
    (*f*) 'Hung drooping unsustain'd' (line 430)

(g) 'mindless the while,/Her self' (lines 431-2)

(h) 'fairest unsupported Flour' (line 432)

(i) 'best prop' (line 433)

(j) 'not Mystic' (line 442)

5. Consider lines 444-72: the irony, the imagery, the use of contrast. How does the long simile which starts at line 445 work? Consider it as an expression of primitivism (the idea of natural simplicity in a Golden Age), and say how far you think it reinforces—or qualifies—the picture of Paradise. Does the thought in lines 445-6 seem original? What, in particular, is the effect of comparing Satan to a rural swain? How is the idea of treachery developed in these lines? How do the lines convey the power of innocence? Consider the description of Satan's reaction to the sight of Eve. Are we made to feel that he might be converted? Or does this embody Milton's insight into what damnation means? Do you feel any kind of sympathy with Satan himself?

Consider the precise implications of:

(a) 'populous' (line 445)

(b) 'What pleasing seemd, for her now pleases more' (line 453)

(c) 'sweet recess' (line 456)

(d) 'thus alone' (line 457)

(e) 'her Heav'nly forme/Angelic' (lines 457-8)

(f) 'That space the Evil one abstracted stood
From his own evil, and for the time remaind
Stupidly good' (lines 463-5)

(g) 'disarmd' (line 465)

(h) 'the hot Hell that alwayes in him burnes',
Though in mid Heav'n' (lines 467-8)

(i) 'pleasure not for him ordaind' (line 470)

6. If you have read all of 'Paradise Lost', or all of Book IX, how do you think this passage relates to the poem's larger structure?

Exercise
13

Milton's *'Paradise Lost'*, Book IV, lines 288-324

Two of farr nobler shape erect and tall,
Godlike erect, with Native Honour clad
290 In naked Majestie seemd Lords of all,
And worthie seemd, for in thir looks Divine
The image of thir glorious Maker shon,
Truth, Wisdom, Sanctitude severe and pure,
Severe, but in true filial freedom plac't;
295 Whence true autoritie in men; though both
Not equal, as thir sex not equal seemd;
For contemplation hee and valour formd,
For softness shee and sweet attractive grace,
Hee for God onely, shee for God in him:
300 His fair large Front and Eye sublime declar'd
Absolute rule; and Hyacinthin Locks
Round from his parted forelock manly hung
Clustring, but not beneath his shoulders broad:
Shee as a vail down to the slender waste
305 Her unadorned gold'n tresses wore
Dissheveld, but in wanton ringlets wav'd
As the Vine curles her tendrils, which impli'd
Subjection, but requir'd with gentle sway,
And by her yeilded, by him best receivd,
310 Yeilded with coy submission, modest pride,
And sweet reluctant amorous delay.
Nor those mysterious parts were then conceald,
Then was not guiltie shame, dishonest shame

Of Natures works, honor dishonorable,
315 Sin-bred, how have ye troubl'd all mankind
With shews instead, meer shews of seeming pure,
And banisht from Mans life his happiest life,
Simplicitie and spotless innocence.
So passd they naked on, nor shunnd the sight
320 Of God or Angel, for they thought no ill:
So hand in hand they passd, the lovliest pair
That ever since in loves imbraces met,
Adam the goodliest man of men since borne
His Sons, the fairest of her Daughters *Eve*.

Analyse closely these lines from '*Paradise Lost*'.

Exercise
14

Dryden's '*Absalom and Achitophel*'—opening lines.

1 In pious times, e'r Priest-craft did begin,
Before *Polygamy* was made a sin;
When man, on many, multiply'd his kind,
E'r one to one was, cursedly, confind:
5 When Nature prompted, and no law deny'd
Promiscuous use of Concubine and Bride;
Then, *Israel's* Monarch, after Heaven's own heart,
His vigorous warmth did, variously, impart
To Wives and Slaves: And, wide as his Command,
10 Scatter'd his Maker's Image through the Land.
Michal, of Royal blood, the Crown did wear,
A Soyl ungratefull to the Tiller's care:
Not so the rest; for several Mothers bore

To Godlike *David*, several Sons before.
15 But since like slaves his bed they did ascend,
No True Succession could their seed attend.
Of all this Numerous Progeny was none
So Beautifull, so brave as *Absolon*:
Whether, inspir'd by some diviner Lust,
20 His Father got him with a greater Gust;
Of that his Conscious destiny made way
By manly beauty to Imperiall sway.
Early in Foreign fields he won Renown,
With Kings and States ally'd to *Israel's* Crown:
25 In Peace the thoughts of War he coud remove,
And seem'd as he were only born for love.
What e'r he did was done with so much ease,
In him alone, 'twas Natural to please.
His motions all accompanied with grace;
30 And *Paradise* was open'd in his face.
With secret Joy, indulgent *David* view'd
His Youthfull Image in his Son renew'd:
To all his wishes Nothing he deny'd,
And made the Charming *Annabel* his Bride.
35 What faults he had (for who from faults is free?)
His Father coud not, or he woud not see.
Some warm excesses, which the Law forbore,
Were constru'd Youth that purg'd by boyling o'r:
And *Amnon's* Murther, by a specious Name,
40 Was call'd a Just Revenge for injur'd Fame.
Thus Prais'd, and Lov'd, the Noble Youth remain'd,
While *David*, undisturb'd, in *Sion* raign'd.
But Life can never be sincerely blest:
Heaven punishes the bad, and proves the best.
45 The *Jews*, a Headstrong, Moody, Murmuring race,
As ever try'd th' extent and stretch of grace;
God's pamper'd people whom, debauch'd with ease,

No King could govern, nor no God could please;
(Gods they had tri'd of every shape and size
50   That God-smiths could produce, or Priests devise:)
These *Adam*-wits, too fortunately free,
Began to dream they wanted libertie;
And when no rule, no president was found
Of men, by Laws less circumscrib'd and bound,
55   They led their wild desires to Woods and Caves,
And thought that all but Savages were Slaves.
They who when *Saul* was dead, without a blow,
Made foolish *Ishbosheth* the Crown forgo;
Who banisht *David* did from *Hebron* bring,
60   And, with a Generall Shout, proclaim'd him King:
Those very *Jewes*, who, at their very best,
Their Humour more than Loyalty exprest,
Now, wondred why, so long, they had obey'd
An Idoll Monarch which their hands had made:
65   Thought they might ruine him they could create;
Or melt him to that Golden Calf, a State.
But these were randome bolts: No form'd Design,
Nor Interest made the Factious Croud to joyn:
The sober part of *Israel*, free from stain,
70   Well knew the value of a peacefull raign:
And, looking backward with a wise afright,
Saw Seames of wounds, dishonest to the sight;
In contemplation of whose ugly Scars,
They Curst the memory of Civil Wars.
75   The moderate sort of Men, thus qualifi'd,
Inclin'd the Ballance to the better side:
And *David's* mildness manag'd it so well,
The Bad found no occasion to Rebell.
But, when to Sin our byast Nature leans,
80   The carefull Devil is still at hand with means;
And providently Pimps for ill desires:

The Good old Cause reviv'd, a Plot requires.
Plots, true or false, are necessary things,
To raise up Common-wealths, and ruin Kings.

Questions

1. What was the political occasion for Dryden's *Absalom and Achitophel*? Identify the seventeenth-century counterparts of: David, Absalom, 'the Jews', Saul, Ishbosheth, Sion, Hebron. Consider the parallel Dryden draws upon between Old Testament history and the reign of Charles II. How seriously do you think Dryden takes it?

Can you think of any special reasons why the correspondence between David and Charles II was useful to him?

2. Consider lines 1-16. What is your judgment of the tone? Dryden could not risk offending the King, yet some readers have felt that this opening is strongly satiric at Charles' expense. Why do you think that Dryden begins with the King's promiscuity? Is there a sense in which the King's behaviour is condoned—or even idealised? How is the idea of *fertility* presented in these lines? Do you feel that the poet's robust geniality takes the sting from what is said?

Consider the precise implications of:

  (a) 'pious' (line 1)
  (b) 'cursedly' (line 4)
  (c) 'Heaven's own heart' (line 7)
  (d) 'vigorous warmth' (line 8)
  (e) 'Scatter'd' (line 10)
  (f) 'Soyl ungratefull' (line 12)
  (g) 'True Succession' (line 16)

3. Consider lines 17-42, the portrait of Absalom. What political pitfalls confronted Dryden here? How far do you think they led him to equivocate?

Does the tone change at line 17, or does Dryden continue the

same vein of irony? How seriously do you feel the King is cen-
sured in lines 31-40? Consider especially the charge in lines 39-40.
Does the apparent forthrightness here make one suspect a deeper
censure in what has gone before?

Consider the precise implications of:

 (a) 'diviner Lust' (line 19)
 (b) 'greater Gust' (line 20)
 (c) 'Imperiall' (line 22)
 (d) 'Natural' (line 28)
 (e) '*Paradise*' (line 30)
 (f) '(for who from faults is free?)' (line 35)
 (g) 'warm excesses' (line 37)
 (h) 'the Law' (line 37)

4. Consider lines 43-74. Would you say that Dryden is now
on firmer ground, politically, than he has been in the opening
lines? Is there any reason to think that he is trying to make us
laugh aloud at 'the Jews'? If so, is he trying to arouse our
contempt?

In lines 51-56, Dryden satirises the idea of the Noble Savage,
and links it with the desire for 'libertie' and with hostility to
'Laws'. To what tradition of political thought does the idea of
the Noble Savage belong, and why would you expect Dryden
to be hostile to it? The attack upon those who proclaim 'libertie'
in this tradition is central to *Absalom and Achitophel*. How far do
you think that wanting too many gods, and too many kings,
are linked, as examples of the wrong kind of 'libertie'? Do you
imagine that wanting too many women—the King's promiscuity, in fact—is also linked? Do these lines help your understanding of the first ten lines of the poem, and especially of
lines 1 and 2?

Consider Dryden's account of the attitude of the English
people to the Restoration. Does he regard the 'sober part of
Israel' as outweighing the seditious part?

Consider the precise implications of:

(a) 'God's pamper'd people' (line 47)
(b) 'God-smiths could produce, or Priests devise' (line 50)
(c) '*Adam*-wits' (line 51)
(d) 'too fortunately free' (line 51)
(e) 'Laws' (line 54)
(f) 'Generall Shout' (line 60)
(g) 'Humour' (line 62)
(h) 'Idoll Monarch' (line 64)
(i) 'that Golden Calf, a State' (line 66)
(j) 'No form'd Design,/Nor Interest' (lines 67-68)
(k) 'dishonest' (line 72).

5. Consider lines 75-84. How does Dryden bring the King back into the poem? How does he link his theme with more general political and religious ideas? At the end, to what specific 'Plot' is Dryden referring? The best account of the political crisis will be found in *The First Whigs*, by J. R. Jones.

Consider the precise implications of:

(a) 'moderate' (line 75)
(b) 'byast Nature' (line 79)
(c) 'Good old Cause' (line 82)
(d) 'raise up Common-wealths, and ruin Kings' (line 84).

6. Consider the syntax and diction of this passage. How does it compare with the passages from Milton you have studied? Does it strike you as being at all close to prose? Would you say that the imagery is deliberately limited in its range? What kind of control does Dryden keep upon his heroic couplets? Do you find them appropriate to his treatment of this theme?

If you are acquainted with the whole of Dryden's *Absalom and Achitophel*, how do you think these opening lines relate to the poem's larger structure?

Exercise
15

From Pope's '*Moral Essays (IV) To Burlington*', lines 99–126

    At Timon's Villa let us pass a day
100 Where all cry out, 'What sums are thrown away!'
    So proud, so grand, of that stupendous air,
    Soft and Agreeable come never there.
    Greatness, with Timon, dwells in such a draught
    As brings all Brobdignag before your thought.
105 To compass this, his building is a Town,
    His pond an Ocean, his parterre a Down:
    Who but must laugh, the Master when he sees,
    A puny insect, shiv'ring at a breeze!
    Lo, what huge heaps of littleness around!
110 The whole, a labour'd Quarry above ground.
    Two Cupids squirt before: a Lake behind
    Improves the keenness of the Northern wind.
    His Gardens next your admiration call,
    On ev'ry side you look, behold the Wall!
115 No pleasing Intricacies intervene,
    No artful wildness to perplex the scene;
    Grove nods at grove, each Alley has a brother,
    And half the platform just reflects the other.
    The suff'ring eye inverted Nature sees,
120 Trees cut to Statues, Statues thick as trees,
    With here a Fountain, never to be play'd,
    And there a Summer-house, that knows no shade;
    Here Amphitrite sails thro' myrtle bow'rs;
    There Gladiators fight, or die, in flow'rs;

125   Un-water'd see the drooping sea-horse mourn,
       And swallows roost in Nilus' dusty Urn.

Questions

1. This description of Timon is taken from the fourth of Pope's Epistles to Several Persons, dedicated to Richard Boyle, Earl of Burlington. Look up the Epistles in the Twickenham edition of Pope, and find out any background information relevant to this extract. The greatness of Pope's satires derives in part from his keen response to the social actualities of his day. Discover from the notes in the Twickenham edition what particular aspects of contemporary life Pope is satirising here.

2. This passage demonstrates with what imaginative gusto Pope applied himself to the satire of disorder. How does he express his own attitude to Timon's villa? Consider the contrast between the chaos described in the images, and the discipline and sense of proportion expressed by Pope's couplets.

3. Consider the effects of the following:

   (a) 'As brings all Brobdignag before your thought.' (line 104)
   (b) 'Lo, what huge heaps of littleness around!' (line 109)
   (c) 'The whole, a labour'd Quarry above ground.' (line 110)
   (d) 'Two Cupids squirt before . . .' (line 111).

4. What attitude towards gardens is Pope expressing here? How do his ideas about gardens reflect his attitude towards society? What do you think Pope meant by 'Soft and Agreeable come never there'?

5. The following lines have been interpreted in two ways:

> The suff'ring eye inverted Nature sees,
> Trees cut to Statues, Statues thick as trees, . . .

This could mean that each statue is thick and excessively large; it could also mean that the innumerable statues seem like a thickly crowded wood. Which interpretation first occurred to you? Do you think both interpretations could contribute to Pope's intended effects?

6. Who were Amphitrite and Nilus?

7. Pope's sense of proportion is expressed by his urbanity of tone, and by the ironic detachment of his wit. Say where you think this urbanity of tone is particularly noticeable. Discuss Pope's wit.

8. Read the rest of this Epistle, and look up William Empson's famous analysis of some lines from the Epistle in his *Seven Types of Ambiguity*. Also look up F. R. Leavis' comments on Pope in *Revaluation*.

9. In the following lines Pope satirises a false kind of order:

> His Gardens next your admiration call,
> On ev'ry side you look, behold the Wall!

From your reading of Pope, try to work out what was his own conception of civilised order.

10. Consider the effect produced by the final couplet.

Exercise 16

(a) From Dryden's '*Absalom and Achitophel*', lines 543–568

> Some of their Chiefs were Princes of the Land:
> In the first Rank of these did *Zimri* stand:
> 545 A man so various, that he seem'd to be
> Not one, but all Mankinds Epitome.
> Stiff in Opinions, always in the wrong;
> Was every thing by starts, and nothing long:
> But, in the course of one revolving Moon,

550 Was Chymist, Fidler, States-Man, and Buffoon:
Then all for Women, Painting, Rhiming, Drinking;
Besides ten thousand freaks that dy'd in thinking.
Blest Madman, who coud every hour employ,
With something New to wish, or to enjoy!

555 Rayling and praising were his usual Theams;
And both (to shew his Judgment) in Extreams:
So over Violent, or over Civil,
That every man, with him, was God or Devil.
In squandring Wealth was his peculiar Art:

560 Nothing went unrewarded, but Desert.
Begger'd by Fools, whom still he found too late:
He had his Jest, and they had his Estate.
He laught himself from Court, then sought Relief
By forming Parties, but coud ne're be Chief:

565 For, spight of him, the weight of Business fell
On *Absalom* and wise *Achitophel*:
Thus, wicked but in will, of means bereft,
He left not Faction, but of that was left.

(b) From Pope's '*Epistle to Dr. Arbuthnot*', lines 305-333

305 Let *Sporus* tremble—'What? that Thing of silk,
Sporus, that mere white Curd of Ass's milk?
Satire or Sense alas! can *Sporus* feel?
Who breaks a Butterfly upon a Wheel?'
Yet let me flap this Bug with gilded wings,

310 This painted Child of Dirt that stinks and stings;
Whose Buzz the Witty and the Fair annoys,
Yet Wit ne'er tastes, and Beauty ne'er enjoys,
So well-bred Spaniels civilly delight
In mumbling of the Game they dare not bite.

315 Eternal Smiles his Emptiness betray,
As shallow streams run dimpling all the way.

Whether in florid Impotence he speaks,
And, as the Prompter breathes, the Puppet squeaks;
Or at the Ear of *Eve*, familiar Toad,
320 Half Froth, half Venom, spits himself abroad,
In Puns, or Politicks, or Tales, or Lyes,
Or Spite, or Smut, or Rymes, or Blasphemies.
His Wit all see-saw between *that* and *this*,
Now high, now low, now Master up, now Miss,
325 And he himself one vile Antithesis.
Amphibious Thing! that acting either Part,
The trifling Head, or the corrupted Heart!
Fop at the Toilet, Flatt'rer at the Board,
Now trips a Lady, and now struts a Lord.
330 *Eve's* Tempter thus the Rabbins have exprest,
A Cherub's face, a Reptile all the rest;
Beauty that shocks you, Parts that none will trust,
Wit that can creep, and Pride that licks the dust.

Compare and contrast these two satiric portraits.

Exercise
17

Thomson's '*Winter*', lines 106-52. (From *The Seasons*.)

106 Nature! great parent! whose unceasing hand
Rolls round the Seasons of the changeful year!
How mighty, how majestic, are thy works!
With what a pleasing dread they swell the soul,
110 That sees astonish'd,—and astonish'd sings!
Ye too, ye winds, that now begin to blow
With boisterous sweep! I raise my voice to you.

Where are your stores, ye powerful beings! say,
Where your aerial magazines reserved,
115 To swell the brooding terrors of the storm?
In what far-distant region of the sky,
Hush'd in deep silence, sleep ye when 'tis calm?
　　When from the pallid sky the Sun descends,
With many a spot, that o'er his glaring orb
120 Uncertain wanders, stain'd; red fiery streaks
Begin to flush around. The reeling clouds
Stagger with dizzy poise, as doubting yet
Which master to obey; while, rising slow,
Blank, in the leaden-colour'd East, the Moon
125 Wears a wan circle round her blunted horns.
Seen through the turbid, fluctuating air,
The stars obtuse emit a shivering ray;
Or frequent seem to shoot athwart the gloom,
And long behind them trail the whitening blaze.
130 Snatch'd in short eddies, plays the wither'd leaf;
And on the flood the dancing feather floats.
With broaden'd nostrils to the sky upturn'd,
The conscious heifer snuffs the stormy gale.
Even as the matron, at her nightly task,
135 With pensive labour draws the flaxen thread,
The wasted taper and the crackling flame
Foretell the blast. But chief the plumy race,
The tenants of the sky, its changes speak.
Retiring from the downs, where all day long
140 They pick'd their scanty fare, a blackening train
Of clamorous rooks thick urge their weary flight,
And seek the closing shelter of the grove.
Assiduous, in his bower, the wailing owl
Plies his sad song. The cormorant on high
145 Wheels from the deep, and screams along the land.
Loud shrieks the soaring hern; and with wild wing

The circling sea-fowl cleave the flaky clouds.
Ocean, unequal press'd, with broken tide
And blind commotion heaves; while from the shore,
150　Eat into caverns by the restless wave
And forest-rustling mountain, comes a voice,
That, solemn sounding, bids the world prepare.

Questions

1. Consider the adaptation of Miltonic (and heroic) blank verse to a pastoral theme. How close is the style to the theme?

2. How do you think the poet conceives this role? What is the implied relationship between himself and his readers? How would you describe his tone?

3. Professor Willey has written in *The Eighteenth-Century Background* of the progressive 'divinization of Nature' in the eighteenth century. Do you find any evidence in this passage of a 'religion' of Nature? Does it in any way foreshadow the English Romantic poets?

4. Consider the use of adjectives in this passage. How effective is it?

5. Consider the poet's powers of visual description. Does this remind you of any other kinds of eighteenth-century poetry?

6. How does the simile in lines 134-137 relate to the passage as a whole?

7. Consider the poet's attitude to birds and animals. Does the stylisation help or hinder the total effect? Would you agree or disagree with a critic who called this 'sentimental'? Does it seem to reflect a secure and certain place in creation for the human observer?

8. Consider the precise implications of:
   (a) 'Rolls round' (line 107)
   (b) 'pleasing dread' (line 109)
   (c) 'raise my voice' (line 112)
   (d) 'stores,' (line 113)

(e) 'aerial magazines' (line 114)
(f) 'dizzy poise' (line 122)
(g) 'Which master' (line 123)
(h) 'obtuse' (line 127)
(i) 'conscious heifer' (line 133)
(j) 'tenants' (line 138)
(k) 'Retiring' (line 139)
(l) 'blind commotion' (line 149)
(m) 'Eat' (line 150)
(n) . . . 'comes a voice,
    That, solemn sounding, bids the world prepare'
                        (lines 151-2)

Exercise
18

Gray's '*Elegy Written in a Country Church-yard*'.

1 The Curfew tolls the knell of parting day,
    The lowing herd wind slowly o'er the lea,
    The plowman homeward plods his weary way,
4 And leaves the world to darkness and to me.

    Now fades the glimmering landscape on the sight,
    And all the air a solemn stillness holds,
    Save where the beetle wheels his droning flight,
8 And drowsy tinklings lull the distant folds;

    Save that from yonder ivy-mantled tow'r
    The moping owl does to the moon complain
    Of such, as wand'ring near her secret bow'r,
12 Molest her ancient solitary reign.

Beneath those rugged elms, that yew-tree's shade,
Where heaves the turf in many a mould'ring heap,
Each in his narrow cell for ever laid,
16   The rude Forefathers of the hamlet sleep.

The breezy call of incense-breathing Morn,
The swallow twitt'ring from the straw-built shed,
The cock's shrill clarion, or the echoing horn,
20   No more shall rouse them from their lowly bed.

For them no more the blazing hearth shall burn,
Or busy housewife ply her evening care:
No children run to lisp their sire's return,
24   Or climb his knees the envied kiss to share.

Oft did the harvest to their sickle yield,
Their furrow oft the stubborn glebe has broke;
How jocund did they drive their team afield!
28   How bow'd the woods beneath their sturdy stroke!

Let not Ambition mock their useful toil,
Their homely joys, and destiny obscure;
Nor Grandeur hear with a disdainful smile
32   The short and simple annals of the poor.

The boast of heraldry, the pomp of pow'r,
And all that beauty, all that wealth e'er gave,
Awaits alike th' inevitable hour.
36   The paths of glory lead but to the grave.

Nor you, ye Proud, impute to These the fault,
If Mem'ry o'er their Tomb no Trophies raise,
Where thro' the long-drawn isle and fretted vault
40   The pealing anthem swells the note of praise.

Can storied urn or animated bust
Back to its mansion call the fleeting breath?
Can Honour's voice provoke the silent dust,
44 Or Flatt'ry sooth the dull cold ear of death?

Perhaps in this neglected spot is laid
Some heart once pregnant with celestial fire;
Hands, that the rod of empire might have sway'd,
48 Or wak'd to extasy the living lyre.

But Knowledge to their eyes her ample page
Rich with the spoils of time did ne'er unroll;
Chill Penury repress'd their noble rage,
52 And froze the genial current of the soul.

Full many a gem of purest ray serene,
The dark unfathom'd caves of ocean bear:
Full many a flower is born to blush unseen,
56 And waste its sweetness on the desert air.

Some village-Hampden that with dauntless breast
The little Tyrant of his fields withstood;
Some mute inglorious Milton, here may rest,
60 Some Cromwell guiltless of his country's blood.

Th' applause of list'ning senates to command,
The threats of pain and ruin to despise,
To scatter plenty o'er a smiling land,
64 And read their history in a nation's eyes,

Their lot forbad: nor circumscribed alone
Their growing virtues, but their crimes confin'd;
Forbade to wade through slaughter to a throne,
68 And shut the gates of mercy on mankind,

The struggling pangs of conscious truth to hide,
To quench the blushes of ingenuous shame,
Or heap the shrine of Luxury and Pride
72 With incense kindled at the Muse's flame.

Far from the madding crowd's ignoble strife,
Their sober wishes never learn'd to stray;
Along the cool sequester'd vale of life
76 They kept the noiseless tenor of their way.

Yet ev'n these bones from insult to protect
Some frail memorial still erected nigh,
With uncouth rhimes and shapeless sculpture deck'd,
80 Implores the passing tribute of a sigh.

Their names, their years, spelt by th' unletter'd muse,
The place of fame and elegy supply:
And many a holy text around she strews,
84 That teach the rustic moralist to die.

For who, to dumb Forgetfulness a prey,
This pleasing anxious being e'er resign'd,
Left the warm precincts of the chearful day,
88 Nor cast one longing ling'ring look behind?

On some fond breast the parting soul relies,
Some pious drops the closing eye requires;
E'en from the tomb the voice of Nature cries,
92 E'en in our Ashes live their wonted Fires.

For thee, who mindful of th' unhonour'd Dead
Dost in these lines their artless tale relate;
If chance, by lonely contemplation led,
96 Some kindred Spirit shall inquire thy fate,

Haply some hoary-headed Swain may say,
'Oft have we seen him at the peep of dawn
'Brushing with hasty steps the dews away
100 'To meet the sun upon the upland lawn.

'There at the foot of yonder nodding beech
'That wreathes its old fantastic roots so high,
'His listless length at noontide would he stretch,
104 'And pore upon the brook that babbles by.

'Hard by yon wood, now smiling as in scorn,
'Mutt'ring his wayward fancies he would rove,
'Now drooping, woeful wan, like one forlorn,
108 'Or craz'd with care, or cross'd in hopeless love.

'One morn I miss'd him on the custom'd hill,
'Along the heath and near his fav'rite tree;
'Another came; nor yet beside the rill,
112 'Nor up the lawn, nor at the wood was he;

'The next with dirges due in sad array
'Slow thro' the church-way path we saw him born.
'Approach and read (for thou can'st read) the lay,
116 'Grav'd on the stone beneath yon aged thorn.'

The Epitaph

Here rests his head upon the lap of Earth
A Youth to Fortune and to Fame unknown.
Fair Science frown'd not on his humble birth,
120 And Melancholy mark'd him for her own.

Large was his bounty, and his soul sincere,
Heav'n did a recompense as largely send:

He gave to Mis'ry all he had, a tear,
124 He gain'd from Heav'n ('twas all he wish'd) a friend

No farther seek his merits to disclose,
Or draw his frailties from their dread abode,
(There they alike in trembling hope repose,)
128 The bosom of his Father and his God.

Questions

1. What do you know of the elegiac tradition in classical and English poetry? Is there anything unusual in Gray's choice of 'the rude Forefathers of the hamlet' for his theme?

2. Consider Gray's choice of metre and diction. In what ways are they appropriate to the elegiac mode?

3. The *Elegy*, like many poems of its kind, is profoundly ambivalent. Gray is seeing the 'rude Forefathers' in two roles simultaneously, both as the happiest of men, and as victims. His own response to them, it has been suggested, alternates between pity and envy.

Can you discover the passages where:

(*a*) The dead are represented as happy?
(*b*) The dead are represented as victims?
(*c*) The poet seems to pity them?
(*d*) The poet seems to envy them?

4. Consider ways in which the poet feels himself significantly different from the slumbering dead, in terms of his superior education and social status. How important is this to what he *feels*?

5. Consider ways in which the poet contrasts the death of these humble poor with the death of great men and heroes. How important is the contrast between these humble graves in the country, and the great tombs in abbey churches and cathedrals?

6. One critic has suggested that the poem hovers on the brink of social protest, but then evades this, dishonestly, by turning to the theme of universal transience. What would you say to this suggestion?

7. Consider the last nine stanzas of the poem—the Epitaph, and the six stanzas leading up to it. Some critics have seen this as a poetic falling off, others as the fitting culmination of 'a context, and a very rich context'. What is your view?

8. Read Cleanth Brooks' chapter on this poem in *The Well-Wrought Urn*. How does this help your understanding of the poem?

9. How do stanzas 14 (lines 53-56) and 19 (lines 73-76) relate to the poem as a whole?

10. Consider the precise implications of:
   (a) 'leaves the world' (line 4)
   (b) 'lull' (line 8)
   (c) 'narrow cell' (line 15)
   (d) 'incense-breathing Morn' (line 17)
   (e) 'rouse' (line 20)
   (f) 'no more' (line 21)
   (g) 'broke' (line 26); 'bow'd' (line 28)
   (h) 'Ambition' (line 29); 'Grandeur' (line 31)
   (i) 'homely' (line 30)
   (j) 'short and simple annals' (line 32)
   (k) 'th'inevitable hour' (line 35)
   (l) 'storied urn or animated bust' (line 41)
   (m) 'provoke' (line 43); 'sooth' (line 44)
   (n) 'pregnant' (line 46)
   (o) 'Rich with the spoils of time' (line 50)
   (p) 'Chill Penury repress'd their noble rage,
        And froze the genial current of the soul' (lines 51-52)
   (q) 'village-Hampden' (line 57)
   (r) 'mute inglorious Milton' (line 59)
   (s) 'guiltless' (line 60)

(t) 'command' (line 61); 'despise' (line 62); 'scatter' (line 63); 'read their history' (line 64)

(u) 'circumscribed' (line 65)

(v) 'uncouth rhimes and shapeless sculpture' (line 79)

(w) 'Implores' (line 80)

(x) 'The place of fame and elegy supply' (line 82)

(y) 'teach the rustic moralist to die' (line 84)

(z) 'dumb Forgetfulness' (line 85)

(aa) 'warm' (line 87)

(bb) 'the voice of Nature' (line 91)

(cc) 'thee' (line 93)

(dd) 'unhonour'd Dead' (line 93)

(ee) 'artless tale' (line 94)

(ff) 'now smiling as in scorn' (line 105)

(gg) 'Now drooping' (line 107)

(hh) 'dirges due' (line 113)

(ii) '(for thou can'st read)' (line 115)

(jj) 'rests' (line 117); 'lap' (line 117)

(kk) 'A Youth to Fortune and to Fame unknown' (line 118)

(ll) 'Fair Science frown'd not' (line 119)

(mm) 'Melancholy' (line 120)

(nn) 'recompense' (line 122)

(oo) 'all he had' (line 123); 'all he wish'd' (line 124)

(pp) 'merits' (line 125); 'frailties' (line 126)

(qq) '(There they alike in trembling hope repose,)
The bosom of his Father and his God.' (lines 127-8).

Exercise
19

Keats' '*Ode on a Grecian Urn*'.

Thou still unravish'd bride of quietness!
  Thou foster-child of Silence and slow Time,
Sylvan historian, who canst thus express
  A flowery tale more sweetly than our rhyme:
What leaf-fringed legend haunts about thy shape
  Of deities or mortals, or of both,
    In Tempe or the dales of Arcady?
  What men or gods are these? What maidens loth?
What mad pursuit? What struggle to escape?
  What pipes and timbrels? What wild ecstasy?

Heard melodies are sweet, but those unheard
  Are sweeter: therefore, ye soft pipes, play on;
Not to the sensual ear, but, more endear'd,
  Pipe to the spirit ditties of no tone:
Fair youth, beneath the trees, thou canst not leave
  Thy song, nor ever can those trees be bare;
    Bold Lover, never, never canst thou kiss,
Though winning near the goal—yet, do not grieve;
    She cannot fade, though thou hast not thy bliss,
For ever wilt thou love, and she be fair!

Ah, happy, happy boughs! that cannot shed
  Your leaves, nor ever bid the Spring adieu;
And, happy melodist, unwearied,

For ever piping songs for ever new;
More happy love! more happy, happy love!
  For ever warm and still to be enjoy'd,
    For ever panting and for ever young;
All breathing human passion far above,
    That leaves a heart high sorrowful and cloy'd,
      A burning forehead, and a parching tongue.

Who are these coming to the sacrifice?
  To what green altar, O mysterious priest,
Lead'st thou that heifer lowering at the skies,
  And all her silken flanks with garlands drest?
What little town by river or sea-shore,
  Or mountain-built with peaceful citadel,
    Is emptied of its folk, this pious morn?
And, little town, thy streets for evermore
  Will silent be; and not a soul to tell
    Why thou art desolate, can e'er return.

O Attic shape! Fair attitude! with brede
  Of marble men and maidens overwrought,
With forest branches and the trodden weed;
  Thou, silent form, dost tease us out of thought
As doth eternity: Cold Pastoral!
  When old age shall this generation waste,
    Thou shalt remain, in midst of other woe
Than ours, a friend to man, to whom thou say'st,
'Beauty is truth, truth beauty,—that is all
    Ye know on earth, and all ye need to know.'

Questions

1. How would you describe the history and the normal appearance and characteristics of a Grecian Urn to someone who had never seen one?

2. This is a profoundly ambivalent poem. Say what you understand by 'ambivalence', using M. H. Abrams' *Glossary of Literary Terms*, the Oxford English Dictionary, and any other reference books you need.

3. What colour do you imagine the Grecian Urn to be? How does the colour green become so important in the poem?

4. In what sense is the Urn a symbol of 'Art' as against 'Life'? In what ways does Keats see it as being superior to 'life', and in what ways inferior? In what sense can it be said to be a symbol (or image) of 'eternity'?

5. The poem presents major contrasts between 'warm' and 'cold', and between intensity and permanence. How are these contrasts related to the whole poem?

6. The First Stanza
   (i) How do you interpret the word 'still' in line 1? Is there an intended ambiguity here?
   (ii) Why 'foster-child' in line 2, and not 'child'? What qualities has the Urn gained from 'Silence and slow Time', and how far are these essentially part of the poet's imaginative response?
   (iii) Lines 3 and 4 have been interpreted as meaning that the art of ceramics is superior to the art of poetry. What would you say to this interpretation?
   (iv) What were 'Tempe' and 'the dales of Arcady'?
   (v) By what stages does the poet's response to the Urn move, in this first stanza, from 'bride of quietness' to 'wild ecstasy'?
   (vi) Consider the precise implications of:
      (a) 'unravish'd bride' (line 1)
      (b) 'Sylvan historian' (line 3)
      (c) 'haunts about thy shape' (line 5)
      (d) 'maidens loth' (line 8)
      (e) 'pipes and timbrels' (line 10)

7. Second Stanza
   (i) Consider the contrast between 'heard' and 'unheard'. Why are the unheard melodies 'sweeter'?

   (ii) Line 5 introduces the first of the two scenes depicted on the Urn which Keats attends to in close detail. It is of two young lovers, just about to kiss.

      Consider the contrast in Keats' address to the 'bold lover' between envy and pity. What does he envy, and what does he pity?

   (iii) In what sense does the penultimate line confirm, or fail to confirm, Keats' 'do not grieve'?

   (iv) Consider the precise implications of:
      (a) 'sensual ear' (line 3)
      (b) 'beneath the trees' (line 5)
      (c) 'bare' (line 6)
      (d) 'Bold' (line 7)
      (e) 'never, never' (line 7)
      (f) 'For ever' (line 10)

8. Third Stanza
   (i) Try to define the *exact* tone of the word 'happy' in this stanza. How does the repetition of the word add to one's sense of its complexity?

      In a recent seminar, one participant criticised the repetition of 'happy' as a structural weakness, and another criticised it as an emotional over-indulgence. But the general view of the class was that both of these criticisms rose from superficial reading. What do you think?

   (ii) Do you think that the main purpose of this stanza is to amplify the previous one? Or does it add something distinctively new?

   (iii) Consider the precise implications of:
      (a) 'happy melodist' (line 3)

(b) 'for ever' (in line 4 twice, in line 6 once, in line 7 twice)

(c) 'warm' (line 6)

(d) 'panting' (line 7)

(e) 'breathing' (line 8)

(f) 'cloy'd' (line 9)

9. Fourth Stanza

   (i) This stanza introduces the second of the two scenes depicted on the Urn to which Keats responds in detail. What kind of religious ceremony is about to take place?

   (ii) In the second part of this stanza, from line 5 onwards, Keats imagines a 'little town' which is not depicted on the Urn at all. In what sense is it made to exist in the poem? How do you picture it, and what *feelings* are evoked? How, in particular, does Keats manage to evoke pity for a deserted, and indeed non-existent town, as a central part of his effect?

   (iii) Consider the precise implications of:

      (a) 'green altar' (line 2)

      (b) 'lowering' (line 3)

      (c) 'emptied' (line 7)

      (d) 'silent' (line 9)

      (e) 'desolate' (line 10)

10. Fifth Stanza

    (i) In what ways does the idea of *coldness* return in this stanza?

    (ii) Discuss the similarity between the Grecian Urn and 'eternity', as this stanza develops it.

    (iii) In what sense does Keats call the Urn a 'friend to man'?

    (iv) The last two lines have been variously described as 'too simple', 'too difficult', 'too didactic', and 'too tentative'. What is your own view? Try to explain how they arise from the poem itself, and what they mean. Do you think that Keats intended to distil a 'philosophy' from his experience or not? May there be some irony, even?

(v) Consider the precise implications of:
  (a) 'Attic shape' (line 1)
  (b) 'overwrought' (line 2)
  (c) 'trodden weed' (line 3)
  (d) 'silent form (line 4)
  (e) 'tease' (line 4)
  (f) 'out of thought' (line 4)
  (g) 'this generation' (line 6)
  (h) 'other woe' (line 7)

11. How important to this Ode is the sensuous richness of the verse?

12. Though this Ode is on the surface simple, it is as tough and as oblique in its technique as many of Donne's famous poems. Does a close analysis of the poem modify your understanding of the word 'romantic'?

13. Read Cleanth Brooks' analysis of the Ode in his book *The Well-Wrought Urn*. In what ways does this further clarify your response to the poem? Consider in what ways (if any) you disagree with it.

14. Can you find any passages in Keats' letters which might help your understanding of this Ode?

15. Write a critique of either Keats' *Ode to a Nightingale*, or his *Ode on Melancholy*, or his *Ode to Autumn*, comparing and contrasting it with the *Ode on a Grecian Urn*.

Exercise
20

Shelley's '*Music, when soft voices die*'.

Music, when soft voices die,
Vibrates in the memory—
Odours, when sweet violets sicken,
Live within the sense they quicken.

Rose leaves, when the rose is dead,
Are heaped for the belovèd's bed;
And so thy thoughts, when thou art gone,
Love itself shall slumber on.

Questions

1. In this lyric three illustrations lead to a conclusion in the final couplet. Is this conclusion a logical development from the previous illustrations?

2. What does 'thy thoughts' mean? To what or whom does 'Love' refer? Is Love slumbering on 'the thoughts'? If so, what does this mean?

3. There seems to be a connection between 'bed' in line six and 'slumber' in line eight. Is there any real connection in meaning?

4. F. R. Leavis argues that in his lyrics Shelley endeavours to create a satisfying association of feelings, but that in so doing he makes no effort to connect his emotions to actual events, or to think rationally:

The poetry induces—depends for its success on inducing—a kind of attention that doesn't bring the critical intelligence into play: the imagery feels right, the associations work appropriately, if (as it takes conscious resistance not to do) one accepts the immediate feeling and doesn't slow down to think.

Do you think this criticism applies to this poem?

5. What impression do you gain from 'soft voices'? Do you think this image is richly evocative, or vague and imprecise?

6. In his *Defence of Poetry* Shelley wrote that 'when composition begins, inspiration is already on the decline, and the most glorious poetry that has ever been communicated to the world is probably a feeble shadow of the original conceptions of the poet . . .'. Does this help you to understand the technique of this poem?

7. This lyric depends for its success on certain musical effects. Note the use of alliteration, the choice of consonants, the rhythm and rhyme scheme. Do you think the music of the poem can be analysed?

8. It has been said that the images of this poem express most precisely the indistinct impressions of the memory. Do you agree?

9. Discuss the words 'vibrates' and 'quicken'. What effect is Shelley trying to create?

10. Do you think this is the type of short, simple poem that does not need analysis, and disproves our argument (see page 13) that all great poems are made more enjoyable by practical criticism? Or do you think that practical criticism helps here as well?

11. Do you think this is a successful poem?

Exercise
21

Wordsworth's '*The Solitary Reaper*'.

Behold her, single in the field,
Yon solitary Highland Lass!
Reaping and singing by herself;
Stop here, or gently pass!
Alone she cuts and binds the grain,
And sings a melancholy strain;
O listen! for the Vale profound
Is overflowing with the sound.

No Nightingale did ever chaunt
More welcome notes to weary bands
Of travellers in some shady haunt,
Among Arabian sands:
A voice so thrilling ne'er was heard
In spring-time from the Cuckoo-bird,
Breaking the silence of the seas
Among the farthest Hebrides.

Will no one tell me what she sings?
Perhaps the plaintive numbers flow
For old, unhappy, far-off things,
And battles long ago:
Or is it some more humble lay,
Familiar matter of to-day?
Some natural sorrow, loss, or pain,
That has been, and may be again?

Whate'er the theme, the Maiden sang
As if her song could have no ending;
I saw her singing at her work,
And o'er the sickle bending;
I listen'd, motionless and still;
And, as I mounted up the hill,
The music in my heart I bore,
Long after it was heard no more.

Analyse (or discuss) this poem.

Exercise
22

(a) Tennyson's 'Ulysses'.

1 It little profits that an idle king,
    By this still hearth, among these barren crags,
    Match'd with an aged wife, I mete and dole
    Unequal laws unto a savage race,
5 That hoard, and sleep, and feed, and know not me.
    I cannot rest from travel: I will drink
    Life to the lees: all times I have enjoy'd
    Greatly, have suffer'd greatly, both with those
    That loved me, and alone; on shore, and when
10 Thro' scudding drifts the rainy Hyades
    Vext the dim sea: I am become a name;
    For always roaming with a hungry heart.
    Much have I seen and known; cities of men
    And manners, climates, councils, governments,
15 Myself not least, but honour'd of them all;

And drunk delight of battle with my peers,
Far on the ringing plains of windy Troy.
I am a part of all that I have met;
Yet all experience is an arch wherethro'
20 Gleams that untravell'd world, whose margin fades
For ever and for ever when I move.
How dull it is to pause, to make an end,
To rust unburnish'd, not to shine in use!
As tho' to breathe were life. Life piled on life
25 Were all too little, and of one to me
Little remains: but every hour is saved
From that eternal silence, something more,
A bringer of new things; and vile it were
For some three suns to store and hoard myself,
30 And this gray spirit yearning in desire
To follow knowledge like a sinking star,
Beyond the utmost bound of human thought.

　　This is my son, mine own Telemachus,
To whom I leave the sceptre and the isle—
35 Well-loved of me, discerning to fulfil
This labour, by slow prudence to make mild
A rugged people, and thro' soft degrees
Subdue them to the useful and the good.
Most blameless is he, centred in the sphere
40 Of common duties, decent not to fail
In offices of tenderness, and pay
Meet adoration to my household gods,
When I am gone. He works his work, I mine.

　　There lies the port; the vessel puffs her sail:
45 There gloom the dark broad seas. My mariners,
Souls that have toil'd, and wrought, and thought with me—
That ever with a frolic welcome took
The thunder and the sunshine, and opposed
Free hearts, free foreheads—you and I are old;

50 Old age hath yet his honour and his toil;
Death closes all: but something ere the end,
Some work of noble note, may yet be done,
Not unbecoming men that strove with Gods.
The lights begin to twinkle from the rocks:
55 The long day wanes: the slow moon climbs: the deep
Moans round with many voices. Come, my friends,
'Tis not too late to seek a newer world.
Push off, and sitting well in order smite
The sounding furrows; for my purpose holds
60 To sail beyond the sunset, and the baths
Of all the western stars, until I die.
It may be that the gulfs will wash us down:
It may be we shall touch the Happy Isles,
And see the great Achilles, whom we knew.
65 Tho' much is taken, much abides; and tho'
We are not now that strength which in old days
Moved earth and heaven; that which we are, we are;
One equal temper of heroic hearts,
Made weak by time and fate, but strong in will
70 To strive, to seek, to find, and not to yield.

(b) Browning's '*My Last Duchess*'.

Ferrara

1 That's my last Duchess painted on the wall,
Looking as if she were alive. I call
That piece a wonder, now: Frà Pandolf's hands
Worked busily a day, and there she stands.
5 Will't please you sit and look at her? I said
'Frà Pandolf' by design, for never read
Strangers like you that pictured countenance,
The depth and passion of its earnest glance,
But to myself they turned (since none puts by

10 The curtain I have drawn for you, but I)
And seemed as they would ask me, if they durst,
How such a glance came there; so, not the first
Are you to turn and ask thus. Sir,—'twas not
Her husband's presence only, called that spot

15 Of joy into the Duchess' cheek: perhaps
Frà Pandolf chanced to say 'Her mantle laps
Over my lady's wrist too much,' or 'Paint
Must never hope to reproduce the faint
Half-flush that dies along her throat:' such stuff

20 Was courtesy, she thought,.and cause enough
For calling up that spot of joy. She had
A heart—how shall I say?—too soon made glad,
Too easily impressed; she liked what-e'er
She looked on, and her looks went everywhere.

25 Sir, 'twas all one! My favour at her breast,
The dropping of the daylight in the West,
The bough of cherries some officious fool
Broke in the orchard for her, the white mule
She rode with round the terrace—all and each

30 Would draw from her alike the approving speech,
Or blush, at least. She thanked men,—good! but thanked
Somehow—I know not how—as if she ranked
My gift of a nine-hundred-years-old name
With anybody's gift. Who'd stoop to blame

35 This sort of trifling? Even had you skill
In speech—(which I have not)—to make your will
Quite clear to such an one, and say, 'Just this
Or that in you disgusts me; here you miss,
Or there exceed the mark'—and if she let

40 Herself be lessoned so, nor plainly set
Her wits to yours, forsooth, and made excuse,
—E'en then would be some stooping; and I choose
Never to stoop. Oh sir, she smiled, no doubt,

Whene'er I passed her; but who passed without
45 Much the same smile? This grew; I gave commands;
Then all smiles stopped together. There she stands
As if alive. Will't please you rise? We'll meet
The company below, then. I repeat,
The Count your master's known munificence
50 Is ample warrant that no just pretence
Of mine for dowry will be disallowed;
Though his fair daughter's self, as I avowed
At starting, is my object. Nay, we'll go
Together down, sir. Notice Neptune, though,
55 Taming a sea-horse, thought a rarity,
Which Claus of Innsbruck cast in bronze for me!

Questions

1. What do you know of the tradition of 'the dramatic mono-logue'? What do you think were the main influences upon these poems by Tennyson and Browning? Consider the influence of the form on poets of the twentieth century.

2. Consider Tennyson's use of blank verse and Browning's use of the heroic couplet. How far do you think they were influenced by any previous poets you have encountered in this book? Analyse the chief differences between Tennyson's usage and Milton's, and between Browning's and Pope's.

3. Tennyson's '*Ulysses*'.

   (i) Who is Ulysses addressing, and on what occasion?
   (ii) Consider ways in which this poem reflects Victorian attitudes on:
      (*a*) Morality,
      (*b*) Religion,
      (*c*) Imperialism,
      (*d*) Social progress.
   (iii) Ulysses is represented as a man driven by restlessness

(almost as one of the great cursed sailors, like Coleridge's Ancient Mariner). In what sense is this restlessness seen as a blessing *rather* than as a curse?

(iv) Consider lines 54–61. Do you think that what Ulysses
says is qualified, in any important way, by his manner
of saying it?

(v) Consider the precise implications of:

(a) 'profits' (line 1)
(b) 'barren' (line 2)
(c) 'aged' (line 3)
(d) 'Unequal' (line 4)
(e) 'know not me' (line 5)
(f) 'Greatly' . . . 'greatly' (line 8)
(g) 'become a name' (line 11)
(h) 'but' (line 15)
(i) 'Yet all experience is an arch wherethro'
   Gleams that untravell'd world, whose margin fades
   For ever and for ever when I move.' (lines 19–21)
(j) 'life', 'life' (line 24)
(k) 'vile' (line 28)
(l) 'gray spirit' (line 30)
(m) 'Beyond the utmost bound' (line 32)
(n) 'Subdue' (line 38)
(o) 'common duties' (line 40)
(p) 'Meet' (line 42)
(q) 'Free' . . . 'free' (line 49)
(r) 'his honour and his toil' (line 50)
(s) 'men that strove with Gods' (line 53)
(t) 'a newer world' (line 57)
(u) 'my purpose holds' (line 59)
(v) 'Tho' much is taken, much abides' (line 65)
(w) 'old' (line 66)
(x) 'One equal temper of heroic hearts,
   Made weak by time and fate, but strong in will

To strive, to seek, to find, and not to yield.'

(lines 68-70)

4. Browning's '*My Last Duchess*'.

   (i) Whom do you think the speaker is addressing, and on what occasion?

  (ii) Consider the character of the speaker. If you were choosing an actor to read this, what qualities of voice and tone would you look for?

 (iii) Do you find this poem too melodramatic? Or do you think that the poet is expressing a particular, if unusual, emotion with great insight?

 (iv) In what country and century do you imagine the poem to be set? Does the poet make any effort to be precise about place and time?

  (v) Consider lines 21-24, and 31-35. Do you think these help to explain the speaker's feeling—and if so how?

 (vi) Consider the precise implications of:

    (*a*) 'last' (line 1)
    (*b*) 'if they durst' (line 11)
    (*c*) 'as if' (line 2: and also line 47)
    (*d*) 'disgusts' (line 38)
    (*e*) 'exceed the mark' (line 39)
    (*f*) 'some stooping' (line 42)
    (*g*)   'Notice Neptune, though,
        Taming a sea-horse, thought a rarity' . . .

(lines 54-55)

5. Do you think that one of these poems is more successful than the other? Explain your judgment.

Exercise
23

Matthew Arnold's 'Dover Beach'.

1   The sea is calm to-night,
The tide is full, the moon lies fair
Upon the Straits;—on the French coast, the light
Gleams, and is gone; the cliffs of England stand,
5   Glimmering and vast, out in the tranquil bay.
Come to the window, sweet is the night-air!
Only, from the long line of spray
Where the ebb meets the moon-blanch'd sand
Listen! you hear the grating roar
10   Of pebbles which the waves suck back, and fling,
At their return, up the high strand,
Begin, and cease, and then again begin,
With tremulous cadence slow, and bring
The eternal note of sadness in.

15   Sophocles long ago
Heard it on the Ægæan, and it brought
Into his mind the turbid ebb and flow
Of human misery; we
Find also in the sound a thought,
20   Hearing it by this distant northern sea.

The sea of faith
Was once, too, at the full, and round earth's shore
Lay like the folds of a bright girdle furl'd;

But now I only hear
25 Its melancholy, long, withdrawing roar,
Retreating to the breath
Of the night-wind down the vast edges drear
And naked shingles of the world.

Ah, love, let us be true
30 To one another! for the world, which seems
To lie before us like a land of dreams,
So various, so beautiful, so new,
Hath really neither joy, nor love, nor light,
Nor certitude, nor peace, nor help for pain;
35 And we are here as on a darkling plain
Swept with confused alarms of struggle and flight,
Where ignorant armies clash by night.

Questions

1. Compare Matthew Arnold's response to 'Nature' with that of previous poets you have studied (especially Thomson and Wordsworth). If this were called 'romantic', would you wish to qualify the term?

2. Do you feel that the poet responds to the scene for itself, or for the reflections which it touches off in him? Is there any point in attempting a distinction of this kind?

3. What do you know of Sophocles? Why does the poet find him especially congenial? What were Matthew Arnold's religious opinions, and how integral were they to his sensibility, as this poem reveals it?

4. Consider the relationship between the poem's imagery, and its paraphrasable 'meaning'.

5. Do you feel that the poem is written to one particular person—or that it is essentially a meditation in solitude?

6. Consider the precise implications of:

   (a) 'Only' (line 7)

(b) 'The eternal note of sadness' (line 14)
(c) 'we' (line 18)
(d) 'a thought' (line 19)
(e) 'distant northern sea' (line 20)
(f) 'The sea of faith' (line 21)
(g) 'Retreating' (line 26)
(h) 'naked' (line 28)
(i) 'really' (line 33)
(j) 'ignorant armies' (line 37)

Exercise
24

Hopkins' *'Carrion Comfort'*.

Not, I'll not, carrion comfort, Despair, not feast on thee;
Not untwist—slack they may be—these last strands of man
In me, ór, most weary, cry *I can no more*. I can;
Can something, hope, wish day come, not choose not to be.
But ah, but O thou terrible, why wouldst thou rude on me
Thy wring-world right foot rock? lay a lionlimb against me? scan
With darksome devouring eyes my bruisèd bones? and fan,
O in turns of tempest, me heaped there; me frantic to avoid thee and flee?
Why? That my chaff might fly, my grain lie, sheer and clear.
Nay in all that toil, that coil, since (seems) I kissed the rod,
Hand rather, my heart lo! lapped strength, stole joy, would laugh, chéer.
Cheer whom though? the hero whose heaven-handling flung me, fóot tród

Me? or me that fought him? O which one? is it each one? That
   night, that year
Of now done darkness I wretch lay wrestling with (my God!)
   my God.

Questions

1. Write a lucid paraphrase of the meaning of this sonnet,
using traditional grammar and language.

2. Why does your paraphrase fail to reflect the dramatic
urgency of Hopkins' poem?

3. Consider all the unusual grammatical constructions in the
poem, and discuss their contribution to its effect.

4. Consider the meaning and effect of the following words:
   (*a*) carrion comfort (line 1)
   (*b*) wring-world (line 6)
   (*c*) lionlimb (line 6)
   (*d*) heaven-handling (line 12)

5. What is the purpose of putting this poem of violent suffering into the sonnet form? How does Hopkins use the volta after
line eight?

6. Consider Hopkins' use of verbs.

7. Note how many questions Hopkins asks during the course
of the poem. Why is this? What questions is he asking in the last
three lines?

8. What is the effect of the parenthesis in the last line?

9. Compare and contrast this with any one of John Donne's
religious sonnets which you admire.

Exercise
25

Yeats' *'Long-Legged Fly'*.

That civilisation may not sink,
Its great battle lost,
Quiet the dog, tether the pony
To a distant post.
Our master Caesar is in the tent
Where the maps are spread,
His eyes fixed upon nothing,
A hand under his head.
Like a long-legged fly upon the stream
His mind moves upon silence.

That the topless towers be burnt
And men recall that face,
Move most gently if move you must
In this lonely place.
She thinks, part woman, three parts a child,
That nobody looks; her feet
Practise a tinker shuffle
Picked up on a street.
Like a long-legged fly upon the stream
Her mind moves upon silence.

That girls at puberty may find
The first Adam in their thought,
Shut the door of the Pope's chapel,

Keep those children out.
There on that scaffolding reclines
Michael Angelo.
With no more sound than the mice make
His hand moves to and fro.
Like a long-legged fly upon the stream
His mind moves upon silence.

Questions

1. The first stanza of this poem describes Caesar presumably at the moment when he is deciding to cross the Rubicon, the second depicts Helen deciding to elope with Paris, and the third Michaelangelo, isolated high in the Sistine Chapel on his scaffolding, achieving in 'The Creation of Adam' one of the supreme masterpieces of art. As you discuss the questions below, consider why Yeats has chosen these legendary or historical moments in time, and what attitudes he is expressing towards creation and civilisation.

2. Each stanza begins with 'That'. Why? The poet demands that ordinary people should 'Quiet the dog, tether the pony', 'Move most gently if move you must', or 'Keep those children out'. What is Yeats trying to say about silence? Each of the three characters is caught in a moment of stasis. What does this mean?

3. What is the effect of the refrain which concludes each stanza? Some readers feel the image of the long-legged fly is of great beauty, reflecting these moments of vital creative activity, when the mind becomes free from the perpetual flow of time. Others think that the fly is a trivial creature and that the image reflects ironically on the pretensions to greatness of Caesar, Helen and Michaelangelo. What is your view?

4. Do you think irony is intended in the following phrases: 'His eyes fixed upon nothing', 'her feet Practise a tinker shuffle', 'With no more sound than the mice make'? Or do you think

Yeats is pointing out that great creative moments take place in very ordinary backgrounds?

5. Caesar is a soldier, Helen a lover, and Michaelangelo an artist. Do you feel that the poem successfully incorporates these three diverse figures in its treatment of the moment of choice?

6. Read Graham Hough's chapter on Yeats in *The Last Romantics*, together with a selection of Yeats' later verse. Do you feel you are gaining more understanding of the meaning of this poem?

7. It could be argued that this poem offers contradictory attitudes towards the hero, at times praising his importance and at others making him look ridiculous. Do you think this is true? If it is true, do such contradictions necessarily make this a less successful poem?

8. Read the analysis of 'Easter 1916' in *Modern Poetry: Studies in Practical Criticism* by C. B. Cox and A. E. Dyson. Do you find that the earlier poem by Yeats adds to your understanding of 'Long-Legged Fly'?

Exercise
26

The opening section of T. S. Eliot's *'Little Gidding'*.

1   Midwinter spring is its own season
      Sempiternal though sodden towards sundown,
      Suspended in time, between pole and tropic.
      When the short day is brightest, with frost and fire,
5   The brief sun flames the ice, on pond and ditches,
      In windless cold that is the heart's heat,

Reflecting in a watery mirror
A glare that is blindness in the early afternoon.
And glow more intense than blaze of branch, or brazier,
10 Stirs the dumb spirit: no wind, but pentecostal fire
In the dark time of the year. Between melting and freezing
The soul's sap quivers. There is no earth smell
Or smell of living thing. This is the spring time
But not in time's covenant. Now the hedgerow
15 Is blanched for an hour with transitory blossom
Of snow, a bloom more sudden
Than that of summer, neither budding nor fading,
Not in the scheme of generation.
Where is the summer, the unimaginable
20 Zero summer?

          If you came this way,
Taking the route you would be likely to take
From the place you would be likely to come from,
If you came this way in may time, you would find the
          hedges
25 White again, in May, with voluptuary sweetness.
It would be the same at the end of the journey,
If you came at night like a broken king,
If you came by day not knowing what you came for,
It would be the same, when you leave the rough road
30 And turn behind the pig-sty to the dull façade
And the tombstone. And what you thought you came for
Is only a shell, a husk of meaning
From which the purpose breaks only when it is fulfilled
If at all. Either you had no purpose
35 Or the purpose is beyond the end you figured
And is altered in fulfilment. There are other places
Which also are the world's end, some at the sea jaws,
Or over a dark lake, in a desert or a city—

But this is the nearest, in place and time,
40 Now and in England.

       If you came this way,
Taking any route, starting from anywhere,
At any time or at any season,
It would always be the same: you would have to put off
45 Sense and notion. You are not here to verify,
Instruct yourself, or inform curiosity
Or carry report. You are here to kneel
Where prayer has been valid. And prayer is more
Than an order of words, the conscious occupation
50 Of the praying mind, or the sound of the voice praying.
And what the dead had no speech for, when living,
They can tell you, being dead: the communication
Of the dead is tongued with fire beyond the language of
    the living.
Here, the intersection of the timeless moment
55 Is England and nowhere. Never and always.

Questions

1. These lines are an outstanding example of T. S. Eliot's use of free verse in its most developed form. They also illustrate his debts to the French Symbolists, and to the English and American Imagists of the early twentieth century.

What do you know of free verse, of the Symbolists, and of the Imagists?

These matters are touched on in the Introduction to our *Modern Poetry: Studies in Practical Criticism*, and in the analysis in that book of T. S. Eliot's 'Marina'. The traditions of Symbolism and Imagism are brilliantly discussed in Edmund Wilson's *Axel's Castle*, and in Frank Kermode's *Romantic Image*. The best single book on T. S. Eliot is still, in our view, F. O. Matthiessen's *The Achievement of T. S. Eliot*. The best book on *Four Quartets* (of which '*Little Gidding*' forms a part) is Helen Gardner's *The Art of T. S. Eliot*. A useful source of notes on difficult passages is Raymond Preston's *Four Quartets Rehearsed*.

2. Where is Little Gidding, and to what events does T. S. Eliot's poem refer? Explain the reference in line 27 to 'a broken king'.

3. Discuss the 'meaning' of these lines, and the relationship between meaning and style. Would a prose paraphrase be less than usually helpful to a student?

Explain what the poet means by 'Midwinter spring' (line 1) and by 'unimaginable/Zero summer' (lines 19 and 20).

Why do you think he writes 'glow' in line 9 rather than 'a glow' or 'the glow'?

4. How far are we given a set of clear visual images? To what degree do you feel that Eliot's sense of history 'modifies' (to use his own famous word) his sensibility?

5. Discuss the strong undercurrent of fatalism in this extract. How do you account for it? Consider also, in so far as you understand it, what Eliot is saying about time.

6. Consider the precise implications of:

   (a) 'Sempiternal' (line 2)
   (b) 'In windless cold that is the heart's heat' (line 6)
   (c) 'pentecostal fire' (line 10)
   (d) 'soul's sap' (line 12)
   (e) 'the scheme of generation' (line 18)
   (f) 'the same' (line 26: also lines 29 and 44)
   (g) 'thought' (line 31)
   (h) 'altered in fulfilment' (line 36)
   (i) 'the world's end' (line 37)
   (j) 'valid' (line 48)
   (k)   'the communication
       Of the dead is tongued with fire beyond the language
         of the living.' (lines 52 and 53)
   (l) 'England and nowhere' (line 55).

7. In many ways, this poetry is unusually 'difficult'. What constitutes the main difficulty, and how justified do you find it to be?

Did you find the 'music' of the verse intrinsically fascinating—even, perhaps, before you began to see what it 'means'?

8. If you have read all of Eliot's *Four Quartets*, how do you think this passage relates to the structure of the whole?

Exercise
27

Auden's '*Our Bias*'.

The hour-glass whispers to the lion's paw,
The clock-towers tell the gardens day and night,
How many errors Time has patience for,
4 How wrong they are in being always right.

Yet Time, however loud its chimes or deep,
However fast its falling torrent flows,
Has never put the lion off his leap
8 Nor shaken the assurance of the rose.

For they, it seems, care only for success:
While we choose words according to their sound
11 And judge a problem by its awkwardness;

And Time with us was always popular.
When have we not preferred some going round
14 To going straight to where we are?

Questions

1. The final line of this sonnet has only four feet. Why do you think this is?

Discuss any other technical innovations which you notice in the sonnet form.

2. What do you understand by the title?

3. Write a prose paraphrase of the poem.

Does this exercise increase your respect for the poet's economy?

4. Consider the use of imagery in the first four lines. In what sense is it visual imagery?

5. Consider the poet's tone. Does he sound too briskly critical of his fellow men?

6. Do certain lines depend for their effectiveness upon epigram?

7. The poem has been criticised for being 'philosophical', and for having too little 'feeling'. It has also been criticised for being intellectually superficial. Do you agree with either or both of these criticisms?

Consider Auden's success in adapting this kind of 'subject' to the sonnet form.

8. Consider the precise implications of:
    (*a*) 'whispers' (line 1)
    (*b*) 'has patience for' (line 3)
    (*c*) 'assurance' (line 8)
    (*d*) 'success' (line 9)
    (*e*) 'awkwardness' (line 11)
    (*f*) 'popular' (line 12)
    (*g*) 'straight' (line 14).

Exercise
28

Dylan Thomas' *'Fern Hill'*.

Now as I was young and easy under the apple boughs
About the lilting house and happy as the grass was green,
   The night above the dingle starry,
     Time let me hail and climb
   Golden in the heydays of his eyes,
And honoured among wagons I was prince of the apple towns
And once below a time I lordly had the trees and leaves
     Trail with daisies and barley
   Down the rivers of the windfall light.

And as I was green and carefree, famous among the barns
About the happy yard and singing as the farm was home,
   In the sun that is young once only,
     Time let me play and be
   Golden in the mercy of his means,
And green and golden I was huntsman and herdsman, the calves
Sang to my horn, the foxes on the hills barked clear and cold,
    And the sabbath rang slowly
   In the pebbles of the holy streams.

All the sun long it was running, it was lovely, the hay
Fields high as the house, the tunes from the chimneys, it was air
   And playing, lovely and watery
     And fire green as grass.
   And nightly under the simple stars

As I rode to sleep the owls were bearing the farm away,
All the moon long I heard, blessed among stables, the nightjars
　　Flying with the ricks, and the horses
　　　Flashing into the dark.

And then to awake, and the farm, like a wanderer white
With the dew, come back, the cock on his shoulder: it was all
　　Shining, it was Adam and maiden,
　　　The sky gathered again
　　And the sun grew round that very day.
So it must have been after the birth of the simple light
In the first, spinning place, the spellbound horses walking warm
　　Out of the whinnying green stable
　　　On to the fields of praise.

And honoured among foxes and pheasants by the gay house
Under the new made clouds and happy as the heart was long,
　　In the sun born over and over,
　　　I ran my heedless ways,
　　My wishes raced through the house high hay
And nothing I cared, at my sky blue trades, that time allows
In all his tuneful turning so few and such morning songs
　　　Before the children green and golden
　　　　Follow him out of grace,

Nothing I cared, in the lamb white days, that time would take me
Up to the swallow thronged loft by the shadow of my hand,
　　In the moon that is always rising,
　　　Nor that riding to sleep
　　I should hear him fly with the high fields
And wake to the farm forever fled from the childless land.
Oh as I was young and easy in the mercy of his means,
　　　Time held me green and dying
　　　Though I sang in my chains like the sea.

Questions

1. Comment on the effectiveness of the following phrases in the first stanza, and trace similar usages throughout the poem:

    (*a*) 'young and easy' (line 1)
    (*b*) 'lilting house' (line 2)
    (*c*) 'happy as the grass was green' (line 2)
    (*d*) 'Time let me . . .' (line 4)
    (*e*) 'once below a time' (line 7)
    (*f*) 'the windfall light' (line 9)

2. Consider the stanza form of the poem, and its syntax. How does the poet achieve his wonderful, lilting exuberance?

3. What is the poet's view:

    (*a*) of Nature?
    (*b*) of childhood?

4. Consider the use of myths in this poem—particularly the myth of Eden.

5. 'The poet's desire is to recreate and to celebrate. One is aware of the adult's viewpoint, but the child's experience is maintained intact'. Discuss.

6. Read the analysis of this poem in *Modern Poetry*, by C. B. Cox and A. E. Dyson. Does it help your appreciation?

7. Consider the precise implications of:

Stanza 1

    (*a*) 'honoured' (line 6)
    (*b*) 'prince' (line 6)

Stanza 2

    (*a*) 'once only' (line 3)
    (*b*) 'clear and cold' (line 7)
    (*c*) 'holy streams' (line 9)

Stanza 3

    (*a*) 'green as grass' (line 4)

(b) 'nightly' (line 5)

Stanza 4

(a) . . . 'like a wanderer white
    With the dew, come back, the cock on his shoulder'

(lines 1-2)

(b) 'very' (line 5)
(c) 'simple' (line 6)
(d) 'warm' (line 7)
(e) 'fields of praise' (line 9)

Stanza 5

(a) 'over and over' (line 3)
(b) 'heedless' (line 4)
(c) 'tuneful turning' (line 7)
(d) 'morning songs' (line 7)
(e) 'out of grace' (line 9)

Stanza 6

(a) 'Nothing I cared' (line 1)
(b) 'take me' (line 1)
(c) 'always rising' (line 3)
(d) 'forever fled' (line 6)
(e) 'sang in my chains like the sea' (line 9)

Exercise
29

Robert Graves' 'A Love Story'.

The full moon easterly rising, furious,
Against a winter sky ragged with red;

The hedges high in snow, and owls raving—
Solemnities not easy to withstand:
A shiver wakes the spine.

In boyhood, having encountered the scene,
I suffered horror: I fetched the moon home,
With owls and snow, to nurse in my head
Throughout the trials of a new Spring,
Famine unassuaged.

But fell in love, and made a lodgement
Of love on those chill ramparts.
Her image was my ensign: snows melted,
Hedges sprouted, the moon tenderly shone,
The owls trilled with tongues of nightingale.

These were all lies, though they matched the time,
And brought me less than luck: her image
Warped in the weather, turned beldamish.
Then back came winter on me at a bound,
The pallid sky heaved with a moon-quake.

Dangerous it had been with love-notes
To serenade Queen Famine.
In tears I recomposed the former scene,
Let the snow lie, watched the moon rise, suffered the owls,
Paid homage to them of unevent.

Write an analysis of this poem. You may compare it, if you
wish, with any other twentieth-century love poem of your
choice.

Exercise
30

Sylvia Plath's '*Sculptor*'.

1   To his house the bodiless
    Come to barter endlessly
    Vision, wisdom, for bodies
    Palpable as his, and weighty.

5   Hands moving move priestlier
    Than priest's hands, invoke no vain
    Images of light and air
    But sure stations in bronze, wood, stone.

9   Obdurate, in dense-grained wood,
    A bald angel blocks and shapes
    The flimsy light; arms folded
    Watches his cumbrous world eclipse

13   Inane worlds of wind and cloud.
    Bronze dead dominate the floor,
    Resistive, ruddy-bodied,
    Dwarfing us. Our bodies flicker

17   Toward extinction in those eyes
    Which, without him, were beggared
    Of place, time, and their bodies.
    Emulous spirits make discord,

21　Try entry, enter nightmares
Until his chisel bequeaths
Them life livelier than ours,
A solider repose than death's.

Questions

1. Do you find this a sinister poem?

2. Is there a theory of art here, would you say—or is there simply a morbid fancy? Consider the effect which the poet achieves by making disembodied essences the active agents of the poem. Does the main contrast between 'bronze, wood, stone' on the one hand, and flesh and blood on the other, gain or lose by this? Does it seem *too* fanciful to create a valid effect?

3. Do you think that the artist is seen as being *simply* diminished by his own creations: or is he in some way their superior? Does it strike you that most sculptors would conceive their role in this way?

Might the poem be more concerned with spiritualism than aesthetic theory? Does its main inspiration, especially in lines 20 and 21, seem paranoiac?

4. Consider the relationship between artist and priest as the poet presents it.

5. Consider the precise implications of:

　(a) 'the bodiless' (line 1)
　(b) 'endlessly' (line 2)
　(c) 'priestlier/Than priest's hands' (lines 5 and 6)
　(d) 'sure stations' (line 8)
　(e) 'blocks and shapes' (line 10)
　(f) 'eclipse/Inane worlds of wind and cloud' (lines 12-13)
　(g) 'Dwarfing' (line 16)
　(h) 'Which, without him, were beggared
　　　Of place, time, and their bodies' (lines 18-19)

(*i*) 'life livelier than ours' (line 23)

(*j*) 'A solider repose than death's' (line 24)

6. The word 'soldier' is reproduced in the poem (line 24), but we have amended it to 'solider' above. Do you agree with us? (The original text is in *The Colossus and other poems*, by Sylvia Plath.)

SELECT BIBLIOGRAPHY

Background to Literary Studies: History and Thought

We have sometimes been asked if there is any authoritative book which would help a student to 'date' unseen passages of verse, or to improve his historical sense. The simple answer is 'no'; in matters of this kind, there can be no short cuts. The literary critic must always be reading as widely and deeply as he can. A sense of tradition comes gradually, and students learn continually throughout their lives.

There are, however, books which serve as a useful introduction to the history of England, and to the history of English literature and thought. The following selection might be especially helpful to a student who is about to go from school to university, or to an adult student who begins the study of literature later in his life.

A. Oxford History of English Literature

The volumes so far published in this series provide a reliable, if not always exciting, introduction to the main writers and trends. The best volume, in our view, is C. S. Lewis'. Each volume has an extremely useful bibliography, and students are advised to bear this in mind when studying any major figure for themselves.

H. S. Bennett, *Chaucer and the Fifteenth Century.*
C. S. Lewis, *English Literature in the Sixteenth Century Excluding Drama.*
D. Bush, *English Literature in the Earlier Seventeenth Century.*
Bonamy Dobrée, *English Literature in the Early Eighteenth Century.*
W. L. Renwick, *English Literature 1789-1815.*
Ian Jack, *English Literature 1815-1832.*
J. I. M. Stewart, *Eight Modern Writers.*

B. Other Histories of Literature

Of the single-volume histories, *A Literary History of England* ed. Albert C. Baugh is the most complete and recent. In addition, the following series may be found useful: ed. Bonamy Dobrée, Introduction to English Literature, 5 vols. (Cresset Press).

C. Historical Background

The books marked with an * are particularly suited to those who have no previous knowledge of the periods concerned. They provide a general introduction and essential historical background material. Those who have already some knowledge of the periods might, however, find the other books more illuminating.

(i) *The Late Middle Ages*

George Holmes, *The Later Middle Ages 1272-1485* (Nelson).
Eileen Power, *Medieval People* (Pelican).
F. M. Powicke, *Medieval England 1066-1485* (H.U.L.).

(ii) *The Reformation and the Reign of Elizabeth*

S. T. Bindoff, *Tudor England* (Pelican).
J. Hurstfield, *Elizabeth I and the Unity of England* (E.U.P., Teach Yourself History series).

(iii) *Puritanism and the Seventeenth Century*

C. Hill, *The Century of Revolution 1603-1714* (Nelson).
C. Hill, *Society and Puritanism in Pre-Revolutionary England* (Secker & Warburg).

(iv) *The Eighteenth Century*

J. H. Plumb, *England in the Eighteenth Century* (Pelican).
Dorothy Marshall, *Eighteenth Century England* (Longmans).
Asa Briggs, *The Age of Improvement, 1783-1867* (Longmans).

(v) *The Nineteenth and Twentieth Centuries*

D. Thomson, *England in the Nineteenth Century* (Pelican).
H. Pelling, *Modern Britain, 1885-1955* (Nelson).
G. M. Young, *Victorian England* (Oxford).
C. L. Mowat, *Britain Between the Wars, 1918-1940* (Methuen).

D. SOURCE WORKS FOR THE HISTORY OF IDEAS

The following works might be found especially useful by more advanced students for purposes of general intellectual background. An ★ signifies works of particular importance.

Hooker, *Laws of Ecclesiastical Polity*, Book I.
Bacon, *The Advancement of Learning*.
Hobbes, *Leviathan*.
Locke, *Essay Concerning Human Understanding*.
Shaftesbury, *Characteristics of Men and Manners* (3 vols).
Eds. Addison and Steele, *The Spectator* (Everyman edition in 4 vols).
Butler, *Fifteen Sermons. Analogy of Religion*.
Hume, *Human Nature and Natural Religion*.
Coleridge, *Aids to Reflection. Biographia Literaria*.
Newman, *Apologia Pro Vita Sua*.
Arnold, *Culture and Anarchy. Literature and Dogma*.
Mill, *On Liberty. On Bentham and Coleridge* (ed. F. R. Leavis). *Utilitarianism. Autobiography*.
Marx and Engels, *Communist Manifesto*.
Darwin, *Origin of Species*.

E. THE HISTORY OF IDEAS

These volumes provide a guide to the main ideas and developments in literature and thought. An ★ signifies the best introductory works.

(i) *Medieval and Elizabethan*

C. S. Lewis, *The Allegory of Love. The Discarded Image.*
A. O. Lovejoy, *The Great Chain of Being.*
ed. James Winny, *The Frame of Order.*
J. Huizinga, *The Waning of the Middle Ages.*
E. M. W. Tillyard, *★The Elizabethan World Picture.*

(ii) *Seventeenth and Eighteenth Centuries*

Basil Willey, *★Seventeenth Century Background. ★Eighteenth Century Background.*
Paul Hazard, *The European Mind. European Thought in the Eighteenth Century.*
Leslie Stephen, *History of English Thought in the Eighteenth Century* (2 vols).
R. L. Brett, *The Third Earl of Shaftesbury.*
C. D. Broad, *Five Types of Ethical Theory.*

(iii) *Nineteenth and Early Twentieth Centuries.*

Basil Willey, *★Nineteenth Century Studies. More Nineteenth Century Studies.*
Raymond Williams, *★Culture and Society. The Long Revolution.*
John Holloway, *The Victorian Sage.*
Mario Praz, *The Romantic Agony.*
Graham Hough, *★The Last Romantics.*
Edmund Wilson, *★Axel's Castle.*
Frank Kermode, *★Romantic Image.*
Graham Hough, *★Image and Experience.*
C. B. Cox and A. E. Dyson, *★Modern Poetry. Studies in Practical Criticism.*
A. E. Dyson and Julian Lovelock, *Masterful Images.*
Calvin Bedient, *Eight Contemporary Poets.*

SHORT GLOSSARY OF LITERARY TERMS

In compiling this short glossary, we have been greatly indebted to
M. H. Abrams' *A Glossary of Literary Terms*. We put these pages here
for the immediate convenience of students. But as we said in our
Preface, we assume that students using this book systematically will
obtain a copy of Abrams' Glossary (it is published by Holt, Rinehart
and Winston, New York, paperback edition available in Britain at 8s.),
and that they will spend some time reading and considering it.

The entries here under such large headings as 'diction', 'form',
'genre', 'metre', 'rhythm' and so on offer the basic facts which a
student of literature must know. But all of these matters are the subject
of long and complex debates. Perhaps we need hardly warn students
that few actual poems are textbook examples, and that very often the
tension between a writer's use of his genre, metre and so on, and the
textbook definitions as they are given here, is quite central to the
uniqueness of his work.

Alexandrine. A verse of six iambic feet. See 'Metre'.

Allegory. A narrative in which the agents, and usually the settings
also, represent moral qualities, general concepts, and other abstractions.
There are always at least *two* levels of meaning: the 'literal' (or 'story')
level, which is often a fantastic tale of giants, devils, battles and so on, as
in Spenser's *The Faerie Queene* or Bunyan's *Pilgrim's Progress*; and the
'moral' (or allegorical) meaning, which is usually a moral or religious
critique of life working *through* the literal meaning. Often, there may be
further levels of meaning as well. *The Faerie Queene*, for instance, is full
of oblique references to contemporary political and religious history.

The best introduction to allegory is still C. S. Lewis' *The Allegory of
Love*. There is also an excellent discussion of allegory and symbolism in
Graham Hough's 'The Allegorical Circle' (*Critical Quarterly*, Vol. 3,
No. 3, 1961).

Alliteration. The repetition of consonants, especially at the beginning
of words or of stressed syllables: e.g. Swinburne's 'Pale beyond porch
or portal' . . .

Allusion. A brief reference to a person, place or event, either in history or in previous literature, which the reader is assumed to know. This is a very favourite device, both of classical poets like Dryden, Pope and Thomson, and of moderns like T. S. Eliot and Ezra Pound.

Ambiguity. In older usage, 'ambiguity' was usually an adverse term; it signified the use of a word or phrase in such a way that alternative meanings were possible, and the intended meaning thereby obscured. In modern usage, the term is usually one of praise. It refers to the *conscious* use of a word or phrase to bring out two or more meanings, all of them relevant. Sometimes, the effect is very close to punning: e.g.,

> There I shall see a sun by rising set,
> And by that setting, endless day beget',

where Donne achieves an elaborate parallel between the 'sun' in the sky, and Christ, the Son of God. At other times, the effect can be nearer to paradox, or to ambivalence (see below).

The most celebrated work of modern criticism in this field is William Empson's *Seven Types of Ambiguity*.

Ambivalence. 'Ambiguity' is a verbal matter, and concerns alternative meanings in *words*. 'Ambivalence' is the term used when alternatives exist in the quality of a poet's *experience*; when we sense that he is responding to the same person, or situation, in several different ways. Often, ambivalence is part of the normal texture of experience. Thus, we are likely both to fear and to admire Milton's Satan; Helen of Troy we may envy, idealise and censure all at once. But there are more complex examples of ambivalence than this; the attitude of Gray to the 'slumbering dead' in his Elegy, for instance (see pages 126-133), or of Keats to the Grecian Urn (pages 134-139).

William Empson deals with ambivalence as well as with ambiguity in *Seven Types of Ambiguity*. Another good discussion will be found in A. P. Rossiter's book on Shakespeare, *Angel With Horns*.

Amphibrach. An unstressed syllable, followed by a stressed and an unstressed: the foot used in limericks as a variant of the anapaestic foot.

Anapaestic foot. Two unstressed syllables followed by a stressed syllable: e.g. ascertain; intervene. See 'Metre'.

Antithesis. The contrast of ideas marked by parallelism of contrasted words or phrases.

Apostrophe. A sudden shift to direct address, either to an absent person, or to an abstraction personified.

Archaism. The use of words and phrases no longer current.

Archetype. The term first became current in the depth psychology of C. G. Jung. In literary criticism, 'archetype' (or 'archetypal image' or 'archetypal pattern') is applied to a situation, or a character, or a plot pattern which recurs frequently in literature or folk-lore, and which sets up profound resonances and reverberations in the mind. Works which make great use of archetypal patterns, such as Lewis Carroll's Alice books, or Kafka's novels and stories, often have the hallucinated qualities of vivid dreams. A great many poems use archetypal imagery with this effect: Tennyson's 'Lady of Shalott', for instance, or Browning's 'Childe Roland', or Walter de la Mare's 'The Listeners'. The images make their own vivid connections, at some level less conscious than that of grammatical syntax or logical thought.

The most interesting modern study of archetypal imagery is Maud Bodkin's *Archetypal Patterns in Poetry*.

Assonance. The repetition of identical or related vowel sounds, especially in stressed syllables.

Atmosphere. The mood prevailing in a literary work. It often relates to the writer's tone, and to his *genre*; also to whatever sets up certain expectations in the reader, so that he senses the distinguishing characteristics of a work.

Augustan Age. In English literature, this term is applied either to the reign of Queen Anne (the narrow definition), or to neo-classical literature between Dryden in the late seventeenth century, and Dr. Johnson and Gibbon in the late eighteenth. See also 'Neoclassical'.

Ballad. A song, usually a short song, that tells a story. Typically, the folk-ballad is dramatic and stylised. Devices such as refrains, repetitions, swift narrative transitions, and (often) a strong sense of ironic inevitability, create the characteristic atmosphere. The most normal stanza form is a quatrain in alternate 4- and 3-line stresses, rhyming abcb. The traditional ballads are mainly anonymous, but there are many examples in English poetry of highly sophisticated literary ballads imitating the form and spirit of the folk ballad: e.g. Coleridge's *The Ancient Mariner*, and Keats' *La Belle Dame Sans Merci*.

Baroque. As in architecture, baroque signifies a heavily ornamented style. Unlike 'florid', it is not an inherently pejorative term.

Blank Verse. Unrhymed iambic pentameters. See 'Metre'. This was the normal pattern for unrhymed verse in English poetry until the twentieth century, when *free verse* largely superseded it. Critics sometimes discern two main traditions of English blank verse, the *dramatic*, deriving from Shakespeare and the Elizabethans, and the *heroic* deriving from Milton. But blank verse has been used by very many English poets, and for a variety of purposes. As usual, large generalisations are very misleading if they are pressed too far.

Bombast. Verbose and pretentious diction.

Burlesque. The generic term for all literary forms where people, actions or writings are made to sound ridiculous by hostile imitation—including parody, caricature and travesty.

Cacophony. The use of seemingly harsh and unmellifluous sounds—often to underline or reinforce the meaning.

Caesura. A natural break falling inside a line of poetry.

Caricature. A portrait which makes a person or work absurd by exaggerating or distorting prominent features (as in cartoons) *without* losing the likeness.

Caroline. The period of the reign of Charles I: 1625-49.

Cavalier Poets. A group of Caroline poets, notably Robert Herrick, Thomas Carew, Sir John Suckling and Richard Lovelace.

Chiasmus. Phrases which are syntactically parallel, but have their elements reversed: e.g. Pope's 'A fop their passion, but their prize a sot'.

Cliché. A once surprising phrase or image, now made trite and colourless by repetition.

Colloquial. Everyday vocabulary and diction. Many great poets have recommended this—for instance, Dryden, Wordsworth and T. S. Eliot. It would be naïve, however, to overstress the 'colloquial' nature of their own best work.

Commonwealth. The period of Parliamentary rule under Cromwell, 1649-60.

Conceit. A figure of speech which establishes a striking parallel between two basically dissimilar things or situations. The *Petrarchan conceits* of our own Elizabethan love poets are characterised by hyperbole. The *Metaphysical conceits* of Donne and the 'metaphysical poets' tend to yoke together violently dissimilar ideas—inside the context, however, of emotions clearly and often passionately felt.

A major study of the conceit will be found in Rosamund Tuve's *Elizabethan and Metaphysical Imagery*. A useful discussion of metaphysical conceits is offered by Helen Gardner in the Introduction to her Penguin edition of Donne.

Concrete. Immediate; particular.

Connotation. The associated meanings which a word in its poetic context suggests or implies; everything in addition to the specific or *denotative* meaning.

Consonance. The repetition of a pattern of consonants, with changes in the intervening vowels.

Convention. The name given to any aspect of a literary work which is generally accepted by the audience. Thus, most literary *genres*, most stanza forms, most types of diction have their 'conventions'. In the theatre, there have been numerous dramatic conventions at different times: see, for instance, Muriel Bradbrook's *Themes and Conventions of Elizabethan Tragedy*.

Couplet. Lines of poetry rhyming in pairs. The most normal type in English are the Heroic Couplet and the Octosyllabic Couplet (see below).

Dactylic foot. A stressed followed by two unstressed syllables: e.g. Absolute; mockery. See 'Metre'.

Decorum. Literary propriety or tact; the doctrine, especially characteristic of neo-classical literature, that the level of style should be strictly appropriate to the character, form, *genre* etc., of the whole.

Diction. The selection of words, the 'vocabulary', used in a work of literature. A very complex subject indeed. There are famous discussions in Wordsworth's Preface to *Lyrical Ballads*, in Coleridge's *Biographia Literaria*, and throughout the criticism of T. S. Eliot.

Didactic. A work designed to demonstrate, or to present persuasively, a moral, religious or political doctrine.

Dramatic Monologue. A poem spoken by one character who is not the poet himself; rather like a soliloquy torn from its context. The monologue usually occurs at a moment of great significance for the speaker—or recalls such a moment; and the main effect is usually to illustrate something unusual, or especially interesting, in the speaker's frame of mind.

Elegy. In English poetry, the term is usually applied to any serious meditative poem, and particularly, of course, to poems concerned with death. The most famous English elegies have often been occasioned by the death of a particular person—Milton's *Lycidas*, Shelley's *Adonais*, Tennyson's *In Memoriam*, Arnold's *Thyrsis*. But the term is used more broadly by Gray in his equally famous *Elegy Written in a Country Church-yard*; and poetry of this kind has much in common with any serious consideration of human transience—such as Johnson's *Vanity of Human Wishes*, or Goldsmith's *The Deserted Village*.

There is no special elegiac metre in English, as there was in classical poetry. But many English elegies have pastoral conventions in common with their classical forerunners. See 'Pastoral'.

Elizabethan. The period of the reign of Queen Elizabeth I: 1558-1603. After the strange dearth of major literature in the reigns of the earlier Tudors, this became one of the richest periods for poetry and drama in our history.

Emblem. See 'imagery'.

Emotive. Often used in the same sense as 'connotative' (see above): the associations, overtones and so on of words, over and above their specific and functional meanings.

Empathy. An experience in which we are so identified with a person or an object of perception, that we seem to participate in its physical sensations. A kind of absorbed contemplation, in which we become, as far as is possible, what we contemplate.

Enjambement. Verse in which the sense runs on without a pause from one line to the next.

Epic. The *epic* (or *heroic*) *poem* is a long, narrative poem, on a serious subject, and in an elevated style. It centres on an heroic figure, upon whose actions the fate of a nation or a race often depends. An excellent discussion of the main types of epic is conducted by C. S. Lewis in his *Preface to 'Paradise Lost'*. The English tradition is studied in great detail by E. M. W. Tillyard in *The English Epic and its Background*.

Epigram. Originally; an inscription, or a very short poem, polished and terse. More recently; any neat and witty statement, whether in prose or verse.

Epithalamion. A poem written to celebrate a marriage.

Euphony. The use of pleasant and musical diction.

Fable. A story with a moral purpose, in which animals talk and act like human beings.

GLOSSARY

Fancy. In eighteenth-century poetry 'Fancy' used to be defined in Lockeian terms as an associative faculty, but frequent personification made it seem almost synonymous, at times, with the Muse.

Coleridge later made a distinction between 'Fancy' and 'Imagination', in which 'fancy' was defined as the more mundane and associative aspect of poetic creation, and 'imagination' as the truly creative and divine faculty. For an excellently clear discussion of these difficult terms, see R. L. Brett's *The Third Earl of Shaftesbury* (especially the chapter on Coleridge). See also the chapter on Coleridge in Basil Willey's *Nineteenth Century Studies.*

Feminine Ending. Lines of verse, and especially of blank verse, which substitute three unstressed syllables for the final iambic foot.

Figurative language. Language which departs from the functional ordering of words, ideas, etc., in order to achieve special meanings or effects.

Often metaphors and similes (see below) are said to be 'figurative'; but metaphor is now often thought to be the basis of all speech.

Rhetorical figures are dealt with separately, under: alliteration, allusion, antithesis, apostrophe, chiasmus, hyperbole, invocation, onomatopoeia, rhetorical questions, zeugma.

Many of the other techniques and devices mentioned in this glossary are also spoken of at times as 'figurative language'. The term has become too large to be precise.

Foot. The basic unit of metre. See 'Metre'.

Free Verse. Verse written without any regular metrical pattern, and usually without rhyme. This is mainly a modern verse form, though there are important precedents in the past. For a fuller discussion, see our *Modern Poetry*, pages 23-27. For a long and comprehensive discussion, see Graham Hough's *Image and Experience.*

Genre. A literary species—or a literary 'form'. The great traditional *genres* were: epic, tragedy, elegy, pastoral, comedy, satire, lyric. In modern times, the term *genre* has been used more loosely to describe other literary forms—the novel, the essay, biography for instance; but these have never been the subject of such systematic enquiry as the older *genres.*

The modern critical debate about *genres* is complex and important. On the whole, modern critics have tended to stress the uniqueness of works of art, and to regard *genre* criticism as a distraction of critical attention from the concrete to the theoretical. But an influential group of American critics called 'The New Critics' have reasserted the importance of *genre*. An interesting recent book is Donald Davie's *Articulate Energy*. But the most outstanding modern contribution to the debate is undoubtedly Northrop Frye's, in his important and influential study, *Anatomy of Criticism*.

Grotesque. A style which shows the natural order in total disarray. Men become animals or plants; the laws of statics, symmetry and proportion no longer hold. The 'grotesque' often includes caricature, but goes much farther than caricature, towards a serious, and often terrifying vision of the absurd.

The best modern discussion will be found in Wolfgang Kayser's *The Grotesque in Art and Literature*. An interesting study of Pope as a master of the grotesque is made by Tony Tanner in 'Reason and the Grotesque: Pope's *Dunciad*' (in *Critical Quarterly*, Vol. 7, No. 2, 1965).

Heroic Couplets. The couplet form of Dryden and Pope, among many other English poets; couplets written in iambic pentameters. See 'Metre'.

Humour. Originally, 'humour' was a physiological term, signifying the four primary fluids of the human body: blood, phlegm, choler and melancholy. The 'mixture' of these humours was thought to determine human temperament and character: hence the 'comedy of humours', which we now associate particularly with Ben Jonson.

The modern meaning has developed from the laughable aspects of such 'humorous' characters. Humour is now essentially anything that makes one laugh. It is therefore a wider term than (say) comedy, or wit, since these words also imply a particular literary style: but humour can be found in many styles, and in various *genres*.

Hymn. A sacred lyric.

Hyperbole. Extravagant exaggeration.

Iambic foot. An unstressed followed by a stressed syllable: e.g. despise; relate. This is the foot most commonly found in English verse. See 'Metre'.

Idyll. A vision of the beautiful and the ideal; usually set in pastoral surroundings; associated with happiness, and often tinged with nostalgia.

Imagery. Basically, anything descriptive and evocative in poetry; anything which helps to visualise or 'realise' a scene or situation.

Sometimes the word *imagery* is used in a fairly narrow sense, to signify metaphors and similes, and the various figures of speech. But often it is used to describe whatever features in a poem help us to make an imaginative response. Thus, critics speak of *visual imagery*, which helps us to visualise, *aural imagery*, which helps us to hear, *tactile imagery*, which helps us to *feel*.

The word 'evocative' is often appropriate; imagery liberates our imaginative insight and response, by bringing vividly to mind our own experiences.

Other subdivisions of 'imagery' frequently met with are:

Archetypal images. See above under 'Archetype'.

Emblematic images. Images which have a fixed, conventional meaning: i.e. violets are the flower of innocence, roses the flower of love.

Emblematic images were frequently related to one another, in medieval and Elizabethan literature, by the theory of correspondences in the natural world. Thus, each sphere had its own natural head or King; and the human King could find natural emblems for himself, as Shakespeare's Richard II habitually did, in other hierarchies—the sun among heavenly bodies, the eagle among birds, the lion among beasts. For a fuller account of this, see E. M. W. Tillyard's *The Elizabethan World Picture*.

Thematic images. Images which recur throughout a poem (usually a long poem), taking on added richness and complexity as the development proceeds—rather like a Motto in a symphony. T. S. Eliot's poetry, for instance, is particularly rich in thematic images.

Imagination. See 'Fancy'.

Imagism. 'Imagists' is the name given to a group of poets whose Manifesto was published in 1913; Ezra Pound was one of them and T. S. Eliot was very much influenced by their beliefs.

In Imagist terminology, 'image' is used to describe a whole poem sometimes, or even a whole play: it is the total 'form' which the poet transfers from experience into words. The underlying idea is that a successful 'image' works so concretely and directly upon our consciousness that it brings to mind the whole complex of feelings, emotions and so on that attended its origin in the poet's experience.

Imagism is discussed in the Introduction to our *Modern Poetry*, pages 10-14. The most detailed critical work upon it is probably Frank Kermode's *Romantic Image*. This, however, is a difficult book. A very lucid exposition will be found in Graham Hough's *Image and Experience*.

Invective. Direct denunciation by insult.

Invocation. An address to a god or a muse, to assist the poet's work.

Irony. 'Rhetorical' or 'verbal' irony is the mode of speech in which one thing is said, and another—often the opposite—implied. This is the underlying mode of satire, comedy, and many sub-divisions of these *genres*, such as sarcasm, ridicule, mockery. It is the underlying mode, also, of the 'mock-heroic' (see below)—and therefore of many of the most famous poems in the English tongue.

'Tragic irony' is the irony of circumstance, conspiring against the hopes and plans of men.

Jacobean. The period of the reign of James I: 1603-25.

Limerick. A humorous poem (often a 'nonsense' poem), written in five mainly anapaestic lines, and usually rhyming aabba.

Lyric. Originally, a song set to the music of the lyre. Then, any poem intended to be sung. More recently, any short poem presenting a single speaker (not necessarily the poet himself) who expresses a state of mind involving thought and feeling.

Masculine Ending. The normal ending for a blank verse line, with a stressed foot. See 'Feminine Ending'.

Masque. An elaborate form of court entertainment, combining poetic drama, music, song, dance, costuming and spectacle, which flourished in the Elizabethan, Jacobean and Caroline periods. The most notable examples are Milton's *Comus*, and the masques of Ben Jonson.

Metaphor. A word which in ordinary usage signifies one kind of thing is made to stand for another. But the relation is not specifically indicated by 'like' or 'as', as in a simile. Thus Donne's,

> She is all kingdoms, and all princes, I;
> Nothing else is . . .

If the poet had written 'She is *like* all kingdoms, and I am *like* all princes', this would be a simile. Clearly the metaphor as Donne uses it has far greater immediacy and precision than such a simile.

Metaphor is basic to most great poetry and, according to some modern thinkers, it is basic to language itself.

Metaphysical Poets. Dryden said in 1693 that John Donne in his poetry 'affects the metaphysics'—that is to say, uses the terms and abstruse arguments of the Scholastic Philosophers of the Middle Ages. Dr. Johnson extended the term to describe a whole group of poets—chiefly Donne, Herbert, Crashaw, Marvell, Vaughan, Cowley. Since then, still further seventeenth-century poets have been included in the list, and the term 'metaphysical poets' is now in standard use.

A great deal of modern critical attention has been given to these poets, and it would be futile to attempt a brief description here. Students should notice, however, that the poets so described did not form a conscious 'school', and did not choose the word 'metaphysical' for themselves. The term in Dryden's original sense is, indeed, profoundly misleading, since the relationship between these poets and the meta-physical medieval philosophers is very slight. The phrase can be best used, therefore, simply as the normal description of a group of poets who have certain important characteristics in common. See also 'Conceit' above.

Metonymy. The name of one thing applied by close association to another: i.e. 'the crown' for 'the king', and so on.

Metre. 'Metre' signifies the recurrence in a poetic line of a regular rhythmic unit. In English, the metre of a line is largely determined by the relationship between weak and strong stresses. Very normally, the rhythm of the reading voice will tug against the underlying metrical 'norm'. The important thing about metrical verse is that it *can* be scanned against its norm; not that it ought to be recited in a sing-song manner to fit the norm.

Accent is the word which describes a stressed syllable.

Foot is the combination of stressed and unstressed syllables which constitutes the basic rhythmic unit.

The most common feet in English verse are:

(1) Iambic (see above).
(2) Anapaestic (see above).
(3) Trochaic (see below).
(4) Dactylic (see above).
(5) Spondaic (see below).

A metric line is called a *verse*. It is named according to the number of feet composing it:

Monometer, one foot   *Dimeter*, two feet
Trimeter, three feet   *Tetrameter*, four feet
Pentameter, five feet   *Hexameter*, six feet
Heptameter, seven feet

To describe the metre of a verse, we name the kind of foot, and the number of feet: thus the normal blank-verse line includes five iambic feet, and is called the 'iambic pentameter'.

For other aspects of metre, see also 'Caesura', 'enjambement', 'feminine ending' and 'masculine ending'. The most recent accounts of metre will be found in T. S. Omond's *English Metrists*, and George R. Stewart's *The Technique of English Verse*.

Mock Epic (or **Mock Heroic**). This is a form of satire in which trivial people and events are ridiculed by being incongruously presented through full epic treatment. The mock-heroic poem is usually a sustained performance, since 'magnitude' is one of the epic qualities being invoked. The most notable examples in English are perhaps *MacFlecknoe* by Dryden (*Absalom and Achitophel* is mock-heroic in parts, but too atypical to be used as an example of the *genre*), and *The Rape of the Lock* and *The Dunciad* by Pope. Many critics would also claim that T. S. Eliot's *The Waste Land* is in the mock-heroic tradition.

Students should remember that a form of this kind is too flexible in its possibilities to be discussed simply. Often the mock-heroic is a spring-board into something altogether more moving and serious than the basic definition would suggest. *The Rape of the Lock* is certainly an example of this. Students would do well to read Cleanth Brooks' fine account of Pope's poem in *The Well-Wrought Urn* as a corrective to over-simplified views of the way the mock-heroic works.

Motif. This term is frequently applied to a recurring character, incident or concept in folk-lore or in literature. Thus, we might speak of the motif of the Fisher King in Eliot's *The Waste Land*, or the motif of the *femme fatale* in romantic literature. In this sense, 'motif' comes close to being a synonym in modern critical usage for 'archetype'. See 'Archetype'.

Myth. In its primary meaning, a myth is one story in a 'mythology', or system of narratives which were once generally believed to be true and which offer supernatural explanations or interpretations of 'reality'. Thus, any religion no longer believed in provides a series of 'myths'.

By an extension of this, the word 'myth' is often applied these days to any *invented* body of symbols or fictions by means of which a writer imaginatively presents his search for truth. Thus, the world of *Moby Dick*, or of Tolkien's *Lord Of The Rings*, or (more mundanely) of C. P. Snow's 'Strangers and Brothers' sequence can be called a 'myth'. It is sometimes asserted these days that men *need* a 'myth' round which to unify their experience; the psychology of Jung has led many to believe that if we do not accept a received religion, then some private 'myth' must be invented to replace it. This, perhaps, is controversial; but in terms of literature, there have been many important writers of the past 150 years who *have* created their own mythologies; and the student will have to understand such mythologies as one of the unifying principles of such writers' *art*, whatever his own assessment of their larger validity or 'truth'. Most of the great Romantics invented their own mythologies—or, as often happens, adapted older mythologies to the meanings they had personally to convey. And most of the major modern writers have also used or invented mythologies.

A very illuminating study of the use of myths in literature since the Romantics will be found in Stephen Spender's *The Struggle of the Modern*. What students new to this topic should bear in mind is that even established myths can be interpreted or used in radically different ways: thus, the myths of Oedipus and Orestes used by the Greek tragic dramatists, the myths of Ulysses handed down from the works of Homer and so on, have been revivified and reshaped by major writers at almost every period of literary importance since they first appeared. Students should also realise that some writers use myths religiously, to explore the meaning of human life, whilst others use them for other purposes: psychologically, for instance, to explore the quality of experience in a character, or a number of characters, or a whole situation. In much great literature, 'myths' are used too subtly and flexibly for one single interpretation of their 'effect' to be adequate.

The word 'myth' is also used sometimes simply as a synonym for 'untrue'. Some critics will talk of the 'myth of progress' for instance, with the clear implication that they are exposing a false belief.

Narrative Poems. A narrative poem is any poem which tells a story.

The form can range from the epic at one end, to simple fables or tales at the other. Many of the great mediaeval romances are narrative poems. Only very simple poems, however, exist *simply* to tell a tale. The narrative poem can often be more usefully classified in some other way—as epic for example, or mock-epic, or allegory, or dramatic monologue, or fable, or whatever it may be.

Neoclassical. The term 'neoclassical' is best used as the name for a literary period. In English literature, it refers to the period between (say) Dryden and Gibbon: 1660-1789 are convenient dates.

The 'neoclassical' qualities are based on the imitation of 'classical' literature. The neoclassical writers tend to admire poise, urbanity, wit, intelligence, 'style' ('What oft was thought, but ne'er so well expressed'). There is a preference for reason rather than 'enthusiasm', excellence rather than originality, 'finish' rather than spontaneity. Nevertheless, generalisations of this kind can give only a limited sense of the variety of neoclassical writing, and have proved a constant source of over-simplification in the past.

New Criticism. The term is specifically given to a group of modern American critics who include John Crowe Ransom, Allen Tate, Cleanth Brooks, Robert Penn Warren and R. P. Blackmur. Occasionally it is used to describe the main characteristic of modern criticism in Britain and America since the seminal work of I. A. Richards and T. S. Eliot in the 1920s. An account of the 'new criticism' in this more general sense will be found in the Introduction to our *Modern Poetry*.

Objective. This word is usually taken as the opposite to 'subjective'; it implies that a writer is presenting his characters, situations and so on as they 'really are'; that he discounts his own personal feelings about them by remaining dispassionate and uninvolved. It is doubtful, however, whether any creative writer ever can be 'objective' in this sense. The word belongs to a very dubious distinction between 'subjective' and 'objective', and usually represents a critical failure to be precise. See 'Subjective'.

Objective correlative. This term is taken from T. S. Eliot's essay on *Hamlet*, where he invents (and defines) it very much in passing:

> The only way of expressing emotion in the form of art is by finding an 'objective correlative'; in other words, a set of objects, a situation,

a chain of events which shall be the formula of that *particular* emotion; such that when the external facts, which must terminate in sensory experience, are given, the emotion is immediately evoked.

This has become, in fact, the best-known definition of the Imagist theories of poetry. See 'Imagism' above.

Occasional Poems. Poems written for a special event or occasion. The poet laureate is often called upon to write poems for royal anniversaries and other public events.

Octave. The first eight lines of a Petrarchan Sonnet. See 'Sonnet'.

Octosyllabic Couplets. Couplets written in iambic or trochaic tetrameters. See 'Metre'.

Ode. The term 'ode' is usually reserved for a long lyric poem, serious in subject, elevated in style, and elaborate in stanzaic structure.

  Pindaric Odes are very formal Odes, imitated from Pindar, and originating in the Chorus of Greek tragedies. There are three parts, the *strophe*, the *antistrophe* and the *epode*. In drama, the Chorus would move to the left for the first, to the right for the second, and would stand still for the third. In Pindaric Odes, the strophes and antistrophes are written in one stanza form, the epodes in another.

  Irregular Odes. These were introduced in the 1650s by Cowley, who ignored the Pindaric form, and allowed each stanza to find its own pattern of line lengths, number of lines, rhythm and rhyme scheme. The most famous irregular ode in English is Wordsworth's 'Intimations of Immortality'.

  Horatian Odes. Horace's Odes were less formal than Pindar's; we should now call them lyrics or songs. Their influence on English poetry has been through Odes written in a single repeated stanza form. The most famous of these are Keats'.

  The classical Ode, as practised by Pindar, was usually written in celebration of a person or event, and many English Odes of the seventeenth and eighteenth century retain this theme. But the Romantics often used the form for some kind of passionate meditation, either upon a natural scene, or a human emotion, or some deep philosophical theme such as the immortality of the soul.

Onomatopoeia. The use of words which resemble—or enact—the sounds they describe: e.g. Tennyson's

The moan of doves in immemorial elms,
And murmur of innumerable bees;

or Hopkins'

Degged with dew, dappled with dew,
Are the groins of the braes that the brook treads through.

Ottava Rima. An eight-line iambic pentameter stanza, rhyming abababcc. This was introduced into English poetry by Sir Thomas Wyatt. Perhaps the best-known usage is in Byron's *Don Juan*.

Oxymoron. The combination of two terms which are usually considered opposites: e.g. 'bitter-sweet'.

Parable. A short allegorical tale, intended to bring out an analogy between the story as told, and some general moral truth. See 'allegory'.

Paradox. A statement which at first sight appears absurd or self-contradictory, but which turns out to have a serious and tenable meaning.

In Cleanth Brooks' *The Well-Wrought Urn*, it is argued that much great poetry embodies 'paradox'. Professor Brooks uses the word 'paradox' in a rather special sense. We ourselves prefer the near synonym 'ambivalence' (see above).

Pastoral. The originator of the form was Theocritus, a Greek who wrote about Sicilian shepherds in the third century B.C. Virgil later imitated Theocritus in his Latin *Eclogues*, and established the tradition for the pastoral: an elaborately conventional poem expressing an urban poet's nostalgic image of the golden and ideal world of the countryside. Pastoral poetry has therefore often been idyllic, and has sometimes created itself around the myth of the Golden Age in the morning of the world. In English poetry, the eighteenth century was the great period of pastoral verse. Many Elegies also have a strong pastoral undercurrent —Milton's *Lycidas* for instance, Gray's *Elegy*, Shelley's *Adonais*, Arnold's *Thyrsis*.

The best book on this tradition is still William Empson's *Some Versions of Pastoral*.

Pathetic Fallacy. This phrase was invented by Ruskin in 1856 for a description of an inanimate object as though it had human capacities and feelings. Ruskin intended the term to be derogatory, but it has since been used as a neutral way to describe this fairly common poetic device. A fuller account of the term, and our reasons for disapproving of it, will be found in our *Modern Poetry*, pages 112-15.

Pathos. This is the Greek term for suffering or passion; in literary criticism it is used of a scene or passage intended to evoke sorrow, tenderness or pity.

Periods. The various periods of English Literature are often given names. Those most commonly in use are:

Elizabethan. 1558-1603.

Jacobean. 1603-1625.

Caroline. 1625-1649.

Commonwealth. 1649-1660.

Restoration. 1660-1702.

Augustan. 1702-1714 (the reign of Queen Anne). But the term is sometimes stretched to cover the whole of the eighteenth century up to about 1789, which otherwise tends to be called rather loosely 'neo-classical' or—much more loosely still, and very misleadingly— 'pre-Romantic'.

Romantic. Roughly from 1789 (the date of the French Revolution) to 1837: Blake to early Tennyson. But the word can be much more generally applied, especially to literature in the Victorian age.

Victorian. 1837-1901.

Edwardian. 1901-1910.

Georgian. This term is usually reserved for the poets who were writing at the time when George V came to the throne in 1910, and who were included in Edward Marsh's famous anthologies.

Modern. The 'safe' dates for 'Modern Poetry' (i.e. Eliot, Yeats and Pound especially; also the poets of the 1930's) are from (say) 1913, when the Imagist Manifesto was published (see 'Imagism'), until 1939 (or a little later, to include T. S. Eliot's *Four Quartets*). But the word 'modern' *can* be used to mean simply poetry being written now; and the 'Modern Movement' has been said by Stephen Spender in his *Struggle of the Modern* to have its origin in the Romantic period.

Periphrasis. The use of circumlocution; in poetic diction, the avoidance of 'prosaic' words, especially as practised in the eighteenth century —'finny tribe' instead of fish, for instance, or 'emerald sward' for green field.

Personification. The description of an inanimate object or an abstraction as though it were alive: Britannia, Liberty, Nature and so on. This is frequently used in epic poems or other poems employing exalted diction.

Pindaric Ode. See 'Ode' above.

Portmanteau Word. The best exposition is Humpty-Dumpty's in *Alice Through The Looking-Glass* when he analyses *Jabberwocky*: it is what happens when two words are fused together in order to get a new composite meaning. The most systematic exploitation of portmanteau words is Joyce's *Finnegan's Wake*. There are sentences, for instance, like 'He dumptied a whole-borrow of rubbages'. 'Dumptied' is dumped and emptied fused; 'whole-borrow' presumably suggests things which are 'wholly borrowed' (stolen) and which have been shifted in a wheel-barrow; 'rubbages' are rubbish and cabbages combined, and so on.

Primitivism. A 'primitivist' opposes 'nature' (especially 'nature' as spontaneous growth) to 'art' and 'convention' (especially in their form of artifice and taboo), and gives his allegiance to 'nature'. The primitivist frequently believes that men lived a more full and 'natural' life in the past, from which they have declined as a result of a repressive and/or an urban culture.

Primitivist ideas were very influential in the late seventeenth century, the eighteenth century, and the nineteenth century, both in philosophy and poetry. They will be discovered in poets as dissimilar as Milton, Pope, Thomson, Blake and D. H. Lawrence. For fuller treatment, see most of the works listed in the Select Bibliography under the 'history of thought' in the seventeenth and eighteenth centuries.

Prosody. The systematic study of versification, including metre, rhyme, and stanza forms.

Pseudo-argument. A train of thought or logic which is not the *real* argument of a poem, but a kind of conceit, offering the real argument obliquely. Thus, Donne's poem *The Flea* appears to consist of a wildly untenable series of attitudes to a flea; this is the 'pseudo-argument'. But the real purpose of the poem is to express Donne's love for his mistress, and his sense of union with her. The pseudo-argument reflects these emotional attitudes at every point.

Pun. A play upon words that are identical or similar in sound but have sharply different meanings.

Purple Passage. A sudden heightening of style, which makes a section of a work stand out of context. The term *can* be used neutrally, but is often employed as a sneer. One result of this is that young writers are often afraid to write richly, or unusually well, in case the reproach of writing purple passages falls upon them.

Pyrrhic foot. Two unstressed syllables together. This foot occurs only occasionally in English, and then as a variant on some other foot.

Quatrain. A four-line stanza, employing various metres and rhyme schemes. One common version is the ballad form, a quatrain in alternate ؛ and 3 stress lines, rhyming abcb. See 'ballad'. Another is the *heroic quatrain*, a quatrain written in iambic pentameters, and rhyming abab. The best-known example of this is Gray's *Elegy*. A very distinctive quatrain of iambic tetrameters rhyming abba was employed by Lord Herbert of Cherbury in the seventeenth century, and later used by Tennyson for *In Memoriam*.

Refrain. The repetition of a phrase, a line or a series of lines at the same point in each stanza throughout a poem. The refrain is a feature of many metrically powerful poems, such as ballads and nursery rhymes, where it creates an effect close to ritual. It was widely employed by the Elizabethan love poets, and also by the Imagists in the early twentieth century. The ability to use refrains successfully is often a high mark of a poet's technical skill.

Renaissance. The 'rebirth' of culture throughout Europe in the later Middle Ages. The Renaissance is often said to have begun in Italy in the late fourteenth century. It did not reach England until the sixteenth century, where it had a late flowering in the Elizabethan and Jacobean periods. But the word 'Renaissance' is too vague to define a period of its own. Many modern historians doubt whether it is a term which can be used usefully at all.

Restoration. The period from the Restoration of Charles II in 1660 until the beginning of the reign of Queen Anne (1702).

Rhetoric. In its original sense, 'persuasion'; and therefore, any devices of speech which are particularly meant to move and sway an audience: 'effective' writing in this very basic sense. Political and religious oratory are 'rhetoric'; the most celebrated example, perhaps, is Antony's address to the crowd in the Forum scene of Shakespeare's *Julius Caesar*.

By an extension of this, 'rhetorical figures' is the name given to any devices of speech intended to give an effect heightened beyond the humdrum and everyday. For a further brief account, see 'Figurative language' above. The various rhetorical figures will also be found in this glossary in their alphabetical place.

Modern usage. In modern criticism, the word 'rhetoric' is often used to describe the whole structure of a work of literature, in so far as the structure is intended to direct and shape the reader's response. 'Rhetoric' is used in this sense in one of the great classics of modern criticism, Wayne C. Booth's *The Rhetoric of Fiction*. Critics of poetry are also coming to use it in this sense.

Rhetorical Questions. Questions asked not to evoke a reply, but to achieve a stronger rhetorical emphasis than that of direct statement. The power lies in our perception that only one answer to the question (or so the writer would persuade us) is possible.

Rhyme. The identity or strong similarity between terminal sounds of words. The use of rhyme at the ends of lines in poetry is normal, especially in the well-known stanza forms, where certain rhyme-patterns are prescribed. See 'stanza'. But poets have also often used internal rhymes— rhymes, that is to say, between words which are not placed at the ends of lines. It is of interest that many modern writers of free verse, who have given up or greatly modified formal rhyme-schemes, have none-the-less made great use of internal rhyme: T. S. Eliot in *Prufrock*, for instance, and Dylan Thomas throughout his work.

Rime royal. A seven-line iambic pentameter stanza, rhyming ababbcc. This is used by Chaucer in *Troilus and Criseyde*.

Romantic. The period between Blake and early Tennyson—roughly from the French Revolution until the beginning of the reign of Victoria. Romanticism was a European movement rather than a purely English one. Its roots reach back far into the eighteenth century or beyond, just as its forward growth reaches into modern times. This is one of the most difficult and multivalent words in modern literary criticism. The student will be well advised to search out its particular meaning in each new context, and to use it warily.

Rondeau. An intricate French stanza, used most often for *vers de société*. The opening words, line or two lines, recur at stated intervals. All rhymes are set by the first two rhyming words. The poem also comes round at the end to its beginning.

Scansion. The examination of metrical structure (see 'Metre'), to count and distinguish the feet in the line.

Sensibility. In modern usage, this normally means our power to respond *fully*, with our feeling and intuition as well as our intelligence, to a situation in life, or to a work of art. In its narrower meaning, it is sometimes applied to the literature of 'sentiment' or 'feeling' of the mid-eighteenth century: this is the meaning which Jane Austen gave the word in her novel *Sense And Sensibility*.

S.. .t. The final six lines of a Petrarchan sonnet. See 'sonnet' below.

Simile. A direct comparison between two essentially different things, introduced by the words 'like' or 'as'. Thus Burns, 'O my love's *like* a red, red rose'.

The *epic simile* is a long, formal simile of the kind which appears in epic poems, almost in the form of an inset. Many examples will be found in Milton's *Paradise Lost*, as well as in the numerous philosophical and descriptive narrative poems which have since been influenced by Milton.

Sonnet. The sonnet is the most intricate of regular stanza forms. It has fourteen lines, almost always in iambic pentameters in English poetry, though other metres have occasionally been used. In English, there are two main patterns of sonnet:

The Petrarchan Sonnet. This is named after the fourteenth-century Italian poet Petrarch, and was introduced into English poetry in the sixteenth century by Wyatt. Its most famous users include Milton, Wordsworth, Hopkins and D. G. Rossetti. The sonnet is divided into two parts, the *octave* and the *sestet*. The octave has eight lines, rhyming abbaabba. The sestet has six lines, and uses two or three rhymes variously arranged—most usually, cdcdcd, or cdecde, or cdedce. Usually, there is a sharp break in the sense between the octave and the sestet, though some poets, including Milton, have been willing to run the sense straight on.

The Shakespearean Sonnet. This still falls very frequently into octave and sestet, but the division is less marked, since the rhyme scheme does not underline it. Instead, we find three quatrains, rounded off by a final independent couplet: abab/cdcd/efef/gg. There is an interesting variant in Spenser's sonnets, which employ a rhyme scheme that links quatrain with quatrain, and octave with sestet, and is sometimes called the 'Spenserian sonnet': abab/bcbc/cdcd/ee.

Modern poets have been less drawn to the sonnet form than many of their predecessors, though there have been at least two very interesting twentieth-century sonnet sequences—Auden's *In Time of War*, and C. Day-Lewis's *O Dreams, O Destinations*. These poets have introduced occasional novelties of rhyme and metre as one would expect, but their sonnets still fall into the two main patterns described above.

Spenserian Stanza. This is the nine-line stanza of *The Faerie Queene*: the first eight lines are iambic pentameters, the last is an iambic hexametre (or Alexandrine). The rhyme scheme is ababbcbcc. This enchanting and highly distinctive stanza, unpopular in the seventeenth century, was revived in the mid-eighteenth century, mainly by poets seeking for archaic effects. The best eighteenth-century example is Thomson's *Castle Of Indolence*. The stanza was later used by Keats for *The Eve Of St. Agnes*, and by Tennyson, for the opening part of *The Lotus Eaters*.

Spondaic foot. Two stressed syllables together (e.g. household, singsong). This foot occurs only occasionally in English, and then as a variant on some other foot. See 'Metre'.

Sprung Rhythm. This is the form invented and defined by Hopkins. The basic notion is that the line of verse should be measured by the number of stresses which in *natural* speech should be given emphasis: in other words, the rhythm of meaning is introduced into the metre itself. Each line of verse has to have the agreed number of *stressed* syllables. It can then have as many—or as few—unstressed syllables as the poet wishes.

Stanza. A stanza is a division in the formal pattern of a poem. Usually, the stanzas of a given poem have a uniform number of lines, length of lines, and pattern of rhymes. In English poetry, there are a great many stanzas which have no name, and must be described for the particular poem in which they occur. But some stanzas occur so frequently, that they have been given names. They are described in this glossary under their appropriate alphabetical place; the cross-references are to:

Blank Verse.
Free Verse.
Heroic Couplets.
Octosyllabic Couplets.

Ottava rima.
Pindaric Ode.
Quatrain.
Rime royal.
Rondeau.
Sonnet.
Spenserian stanza.
Tercet.
Terza rima.
Triolet.
Villanelle.

Stress. This word is used to describe where the emphasis falls; a *heavy* stress is one which the metre and rhythm fall upon, a *weak* stress is one which is 'unstressed'. Thus, the word 'mention' consists of a heavy stress followed by a weak stress. In metre, this pattern forms the foot called trochaic. See 'Metre'.

Structure. The organisation or total design of a particular poem; the 'form' to which all the parts contribute.

Style. The characteristic manner of expression in a poem: *how* it says what it says, and is what it is. 'Style' can be analysed in terms of the various categories which this glossary lists—a poem's diction, its *genre*, metre, stanza form, figures of speech and so on. But all of these things are part of a larger whole. The word 'style', like the word 'structure' (see above), is now usually used to describe this whole.

Subjective. This usually refers to the kind of literature in which the poet projects his personal emotions, responses, insights and so on into his actual descriptions of people and events. In this sense, it is often opposed to 'objective'. But see 'objective' (above). Our reservations expressed there apply to both these terms.

Syllabics. A verse form in which each line has to have an agreed number of syllables. This differs from other metres in that it disregards stress.

Symbol. Perhaps no critical term is more alarming than this, especially to beginners in literary criticism. The normal usages of the word can perhaps be briefly indicated, so that they can be distinguished from the present critical use:

(1) At its simplest, a 'symbol' is any sign which stands for a concept.

(2) According to Locke, words themselves are 'symbols' of ideas; they help us to convey our private and internal concepts to other minds.

(3) In mathematics, 'symbols' are a kind of shorthand for concepts which would otherwise have to be explained each time at awkward length.

(4) In religious mysticism, the natural world is often said to be 'symbolic' of the mind of God. That is to say, the imprint of the creator is to be felt upon His creation, just as the imprint of a poet may be felt upon the poem he has made. A tree, or a stone, may be said to 'symbolise' the divine mind, to 'point towards' a reality greater than itself, in which it partakes.

In literary criticism, all of these usages are comparatively rare, though Coleridge and Wordsworth often use the sense outlined in (4). By 'symbol', the modern literary critic will most likely mean an image or metaphor with a rich but indefinite suggestiveness. In *allegory* (see above), the images and metaphors 'stand for' exact moral equivalents, and can be translated into these. But in *symbolism*, the image or metaphor resonates with suggestions and evocations, any or all of which are relevant to our response. The effect of such poetry is mysterious, but not imprecise. Our characteristic impression is of very concrete images which *release* rather than *contain* their 'meanings'. Visually, and often literally, we are offered a great clarity; only in allusiveness and evocation are we teased with a richness not easily explained.

The origin of modern 'symbolist' poetry is in the French school of the nineteenth century; in the twentieth century, Yeats and Eliot have both used richly symbolist techniques. But it may be that the symbolists defined an element that exists in very much great poetry, of the past as well as the present, rather than that they invented something new. Our modern understanding of Shakespeare, for instance, owes much to symbolist thought. And we are now aware that symbolism is a key to understanding many great novels and plays, as well as poems.

Sympathy. Fellow feeling with another person, amounting to vicarious identification. See also 'Empathy'.

Synecdoche. A part of something used to signify the whole: thus, 'deaf ears' for people who refuse to hear.

Synesthesia. The description of one sensation in terms of another: e.g. Dylan Thomas' 'tunes from the chimneys', where the sight and smell of smoke becomes fused, in the child's delight, with sound.

Tension. This word tends to be used to describe poems in which several meanings or implications are held tightly together in one set of images, or one structural complex. Thus a poem with more than one level of meaning, or with ironic overtones, or with emotional paradoxes or ambivalences, may hold its diverse meanings in the 'tension' of its own clarity and unity.

Tercet. A three-line stanza, usually with a single rhyme, in which the lines may be of the same or different lengths.

Terza Rima. Lines written in tercets, and rhyming: aba/bcb/cdc/ded and so on, so that each tercet is linked, and the poem has the appearance of unending continuity.

Tone. The attitude to the subject matter on the one hand, and to the audience on the other, implied in the structure and style of a literary work.

Tradition. As used by Arnold and Eliot, 'tradition' means the whole body of European—and perhaps 'world'—literature, of which a civilised writer will be aware, and to which he may in his tone, or structure, or use of irony or allusiveness, refer. Beyond this, it means a sense shared by writer and reader of the continuity of certain values and directions in our culture. The tension between originality and tradition is discussed in T. S. Eliot's famous essay, 'Tradition and the Individual Talent'.

Triolet. A stanza of eight lines, with two rhymes. The first line is repeated as the fourth and seventh, and the second as the eighth.

Trochaic foot. A stressed syllable followed by an unstressed: e.g. Faithless, Tiger. See 'Metre'.

Trope. The use of words with a decided shift or extension of their literal meaning. This includes a number of figures of speech, such as synecdoche and metonymy.

Vers de société. Brief epigrammatic or lyrical verse, dealing with the surface events or concerns of polite society.

Verse. A metrical line. See 'Metre'.

Victorian. The period of Victoria's reign, 1837-1901. The word is sometimes extended to cover certain attitudes, beliefs or styles. In the cent past, the word has often been derogatory. Fortunately, this icular arrogance seems now to have passed.

Villanelle. A poem consisting of five three-line stanzas, and one of four. It has two rhymes throughout, and two refrains, which occur in eight of the nineteen lines. Though this form is technically difficult, and usually attuned to elegant light verse, there have been some rather moving villanelles by modern poets—particularly by Auden, Empson and John Wain.

Wit. In common usage, the word now means a brief and well-phrased expression, contrived to give one a shock of amused surprise, and calculated to stick in the mind. But this is one of the words which has changed its meaning in important ways from one period to another. An excellent discussion will be found in C. S. Lewis' *Studies In Words*. The student will discover distinctive categories of 'metaphysical wit' (see 'Metaphysical') and 'Augustan wit' in general critical use. As usual, our best advice must be a warning against over-generalised use of the word.

Zeugma. The use of a single word standing in the same grammatical relation to two other terms, but with some alteration of meaning: e.g. Pope's celebrated line 'To rest, the cushion and soft Dean invite'.